Hans Dieter Schaal

Festung Königstein
Ausstellungsdesign
Exhibition Design

Hans Dieter Schaal

Festung Königstein
Ausstellungsdesign
Exhibition Design

Edition Axel Menges

Veröffentlicht in Zusammenarbeit mit der Festung Königstein gGmbH

Published in cooperation with the Festung Königstein gGmbH

ISBN 978-3-86905-024-9

Druck und Bindearbeiten / Printing and binding: Graspo CZ, a. s., Zlín, Tschechische Republik / Czech Republic

Übersetzung ins Englische / Translation into English: Alison Kirkland
Lektorat / Editing: Dorothea Duwe, Nora Krehl-von Mühlendahl, Verena Schaal, Angelika Taube, Carl Wege
Design: Axel Menges

1. Kanonen auf der Georgenbatterie oberhalb des Eingangs zur Festung.
2. Festliches Treffen historischer Figuren auf einem Spiegelpodest in der Dauerausstellung im Torhaus.
3. Rundgang während der Vorbereitung der Dauerausstellung. Die Beteiligten von links nach rechts: Angelika Taube, Hans Dieter Schaal, Ingo Busse und Melanie Brugger.
4. Die Beteiligten beim Planen: Armin Teufel, Hans Dieter Schaal, Melanie Brugger.

1. Cannons on the Georgen battery above the entrance to the fortress.
2. Festive meeting of historical figures on a mirror platform in the permanent exhibition in the Gatehouse.
3. Tour during the preparation of the permanent exhibition. The participants from left to right: Angelika Taube, Hans Dieter Schaal, Ingo Busse and Melanie Brugger.
4. Those involved in planning: Armin Teufel, Hans Dieter Schaal and Melanie Brugger.

Vorwort
Angelika Taube

Die bereits mehr als zwei Jahrzehnte währende Zusammenarbeit mit dem Künstler-Architekten Hans Dieter Schaal war und ist ein Glücksfall für die Festung Königstein. Der Kontakt kam zur rechten Zeit zustande: Seit Beginn der 1990er Jahre saniert der Freistaat Sachsen zielstrebig das vielbesuchte, denkmalgeschützte bauliche Ensemble in der Sächsischen Schweiz. Die instandgesetzten Räume riefen nach Nutzung und Gestaltung, vor allem im musealen Sinne. Denn diese Festung beeindruckt nicht nur durch hohe Mauern und alte, imposante Gebäude sowie ihre landschaftlich reizvolle Lage. Sie besitzt auch eine lange und vielfältige, höchst interessante und manchmal sogar amüsante Geschichte, die Menschen in ihren Bann ziehen kann. Sie muß nur spannend und kurzweilig erzählt und adäquat veranschaulicht werden. Das betrifft einerseits die Bau- und Nutzungsgeschichte der einzelnen Gebäude auf dem Königstein – zum Beispiel die des Brunnenhauses, der Georgenburg und des Alten Zeughauses – , andererseits aber auch die historischen Ereignisse, Themen der sächsischen Geschichte, in die der Königstein involviert war und die es lohnt, in einer großen Dauerausstellung und in Sonderausstellungen zu präsentieren.

Als Ausstellungsarchitekt und Künstler war und ist Hans Dieter Schaal dafür der ideale Partner: Sein Interesse für historische Themen, seine Phantasie und Kreativität, sein inszenatorisches Geschick und nicht zuletzt seine langjährigen Erfahrungen als Bühnenbildner waren und sind Garanten für attraktive Gestaltungen. Zahlreiche Eintragungen der Besucher in den Gästebüchern der Festung Königstein legen davon Zeugnis ab.

Alle in diesem Buch beschriebenen Ausstellungen sind in regem Gedankenaustausch und intensiver Zusammenarbeit zwischen Hans Dieter Schaal und seinen Mitarbeitenden sowie dem Ausstellungsteam der Festung Königstein Wirklichkeit geworden. Das jeweilige Thema setzte das Festungsteam, das auch die Inhalte wissenschaftlich erarbeitete. Grundlage für die architektonische Gestaltung waren die meist zahlreichen Entwurfsvarianten, mit denen Hans Dieter Schaal in die Beratungen kam. Nicht immer fiel die Entscheidung für eine dieser Varianten leicht, oft wurde um die möglichst perfekte Version gerungen, die allen Ansprüchen gerecht werden sollte – von der Ästhetik über die Mehrsprachigkeit und die Sicherheit für die musealen Objekte bis hin zur Unterbringung interaktiver Angebote für Erwachsene und Kinder. Dank dem Engagement aller Beteiligten stand am Ende immer ein Erfolg: staunende und begeisterte Besucher, die sich in den letzten Jahren auch im Internet immer wieder lobend über die Ausstellungen auf der Festung Königstein geäußert haben.

Den Leserinnen und Lesern der vorliegenden Publikation seien an dieser Stelle ebenfalls interessante »Ausstellungserlebnisse« gewünscht. Vielleicht machen ja Tretrad, Spiegelsaal und Flaschenfaß Lust auf einen Besuch der Festung Königstein selbst.

Persönlich danke ich Hans Dieter Schaal dafür, daß er mir die Möglichkeit eingeräumt hat, an diesem Buch mitzuwirken.

Foreword
Angelika Taube

Our collaboration with the artist and architect Hans Dieter Schaal has now run for more than two decades, and continues to be a boon for the Königstein Fortress. We contacted each other at the right time: since the early 1990s, the Free State of Saxony has been determinedly renovating this much-visited architectural ensemble – a listed monument – in Saxon Switzerland. The renovated rooms were crying out to be used and to be given a design – specifically, for museum purposes. After all, this Fortress is impressive not just because of its high walls and old and impressive buildings and its charming surrounding landscape. It also possesses a long and varied, highly interesting and sometimes even amusing story able to enchant many people. It only needs to be told in an exciting and entertaining way and adequately illustrated. This applies equally to the history of how individual buildings on the Königstein were constructed and used – for instance, the Well House, the Johann Georg Castle, and the the Old Armoury – and to the historic events and themes of Saxon history in which the Königstein has been involved. All of this is well worth presenting in a largescale long-term exhibition and also in special exhibitions.

As an exhibition architect and artist, Hans Dieter Schaal is the ideal partner in this endeavour: his interest in the historic themes, his imagination and creativity, his aptitude for scenic presentation, and, not least, his long years of experience as a stage set creator guarantee attractive designs. Numerous entries made by visitors in the guest books of the Königstein Fortress attest to this.

All of the exhibitions described in this book were the result of a lively exchange of ideas and intensive collaboration between Hans Dieter Schaal and his working team and the Fortress Königstein exhibition team. In each case, the theme is set by the Fortress team, who also develop the content from a scientific perspective. The drafts brought by Hans Dieter Schaal to discussions (usually in several variations) provided the basis for the architectonic design. It was not always easy to settle on one of these variants – there was often a struggle to determine the most perfect version, the one most able to satisfy all the requirements – from the aesthetic to multilingual text and security for the museum objects to accommodating interactive elements for adults and children. Thanks to the commitment of all those involved, the end result was always a success: in the form of astonished and intrigued visitors, who, in recent years, have expressed plenty of praise for the exhibitions at the Fortress Königstein also on the Internet.

We hope that the readers of this publication will have equally interesting »exhibition experiences«. Perhaps seeing the tread wheel, the mirror hall, and the »bottle barrel« will give them a desire to visit Fortress Königstein itself.

I would like to personally thank Hans Dieter Schaal for giving me the opportunity to collaborate on this book.

Einführung

Wer sich für historische Burgen und Festungen in Europa interessiert, wird früher oder später auf die Festung Königstein in Sachsen stoßen. Sie zählt zu den größten und imposantesten Bauten ihrer Art. Da sie unweit von Dresden, inmitten des Elbsandsteingebirges in der Sächsischen Schweiz liegt, ist sie heute als Tagesausflugsziel bei Touristen, Wanderern und Kletterern sehr beliebt. Jedes Jahr kommen eine halbe Million Gäste – darunter viele Familien mit Kindern – und wollen die Sehenswürdigkeit bewundern und »erobern«, wie es in den Reiseprospekten heißt.

Zur Geschichte der Festung gibt es Sachbücher. Vor allem *Festung Königstein* von Angelika Taube, ein schmaler, immer wieder neu aufgelegter Band mit den wichtigsten historischen Informationen, der mit seinen Plänen und Photos auch als Reiseführer gedacht ist. Von der gleichen Autorin erschien 2017 – unter Mitwirkung der Kuratoren auf der Festung und zahlreicher weiterer Fachleute – ein dickes Katalogbuch zur neuen Dauerausstellung. Wir wollen uns daher auf die wesentlichen Daten beschränken.

Durch Scherbenfunde wurde nachgewiesen, daß das 247 m über dem Elbspiegel und 361 m über dem Meeresspiegel liegende Felsplateau mit seiner Fläche von 9,5 ha schon während der Bronzezeit, vor 3000 Jahren (temporär?), besiedelt war. Die eigentliche, durch Dokumente und Gebäudereste nachgewiesene Burg- und Festungsgeschichte beginnt erst im Jahr 1241. Damals wurde der Königstein (»Lapis regis«) erstmals urkundlich erwähnt. Auf dem Felsplateau gab es eine Burg, von der bauliche Reste in der heutigen Johann-Georgenburg enthalten sind. Sie bilden die Urzelle, den Kern der Gesamtanlage.

Anfänglich gehörten die Burg Königstein und das umliegende Gebiet zu Böhmen, erst im Jahr 1409, nach der »Dohnaischen Fehde«, wechselten die Machtverhältnisse. Die neuen Besitzer waren die Markgrafen von Meißen. Heute verläuft die Grenze zu Tschechien nur wenige Kilometer elbaufwärts, hinter Bad Schandau.

Die überwachend-abschreckende militärische Nutzung vom Königstein stand in dieser frühen Zeit im Vordergrund. Dafür war die Lage der Burg optimal. Man konnte von hier oben den gesamten Elbverkehr beobachten und feindliche Armeen, die sich annäherten, schon aus der Ferne erkennen. Allerdings behinderten die Hügel und bewaldeten Tafelberge einen vollständigen Überblick. Täler und Bäume hätten genügend Sichtschutz zur unbemerkten Annäherung geboten. Trotzdem flößten die mächtigen Sandsteinwände genügend Respekt ein, so daß es die nächsten Jahrhunderte über nie zu größeren militärischen Angriffen, Belagerungen und Auseinandersetzungen kam.

Im Laufe des 16. Jahrhunderts mußte der Königstein wegen der neu entwickelten Pulverwaffen und damit der neuen Art von Kriegsführung weiter ausgebaut werden. Erst ab dem Jahr 1589 kann man von einer wirklichen Festung – genauer: von einer »Landesfestung« – sprechen.

Um für die Ernährung der ständig anwesenden Besatzung zu sorgen, benötigte man Proviantlager und einen überlebenswichtigen Brunnen.

Dieser wurde zwischen 1563 und 1569 aus dem Felsen geschlagen, abgeteuft, wie es in der Bergmannssprache heißt. Mit seinen 152,5 m gehört er zu den tiefsten Brunnen innerhalb europäischer Burgen und Festungen. Eine bergmännische Meisterleistung.

Wegen der militärisch bewachten Sicherheit und der schönen Lage an der Elbe und im Elbsandsteingebirge entschlossen sich die sächsischen Kurfürsten im 17. Jahrhundert dazu, den Ort auch als Mittelpunkt ihrer Jagdleidenschaft zu nutzen. Während der Tage ihrer Anwesenheit mit zahlreichen hohen Gästen feierten sie üppige Feste und Gelage mit Wein, Musik und Tanz.

Aus der militärischen Festung wurde im Verlauf des 17. und 18. Jahrhunderts eine (kur)fürstliche Lustschloßanlage. Allerdings gab es im Sinne von Dresden, Moritzburg oder Pillnitz hier nicht den Luxus eines wirklichen Lustschlosses. Ein großer Bankett- und Ballsaal – das heutige Neue Zeughaus, früher genannt »Johannissaal« (fertiggestellt 1631) – mußte genügen.

In den Jahren 1722 bis 1725 ließ August der Starke von Küfern aus Weimar, Durlach (heute Karlsruhe) und Zweibrücken, einem Zimmermann aus Zürich und dem Festungsböttcher ein Riesenweinfaß in den Keller der Magdalenenburg einbauen.

Die äußere Schmuckarchitektur entwarf sein damaliger Oberlandbaumeister Matthäus Daniel Pöppelmann (1662–1736), der Erbauer des Dresdner Zwingers. Das Faß konnte nahezu 240 000 Liter Wein aufnehmen. Aber der Spaß sollte nur von begrenzter Dauer sein. Nachdem das Faß 1740 zum zweiten Mal gefüllt worden war, zeigten sich einige Jahre später (1769) erste Schäden. 1819 mußte das Riesenweinfaß abgebrochen werden. Zur Erinnerung daran und um die einstige Größe des Fasses zu veranschaulichen, entstand 2010/11 unsere Kunstinstallation aus Tausenden von grünen Weinflaschen und erfreut seitdem – bei einer speziellen Führung – die Besucher aus aller Welt.

Im 18. und 19. Jahrhundert wechselte die Nutzung der Festung erneut. Die königlich-sächsischen Ämter in Dresden ließen – vor drohenden Kriegen – Staatsgelder, wichtige Dokumente und Kunstwerke zum Schutz vor Feinden auf die Festung bringen. Ein eigenes, hochgesichertes, tresorartiges »Schatzhaus« ergänzte im 19. Jahrhundert in der Nähe des Brunnenhauses das Sicherheitsangebot. Auch während des Zweiten Weltkriegs diente die Festung als sicheres Kunstdepot.

Schon seit dem späten 16. Jahrhundert wurden außerdem einzelne Festungsgebäude zum gefürchteten Staatsgefängnis (Festungshaft) umfunktioniert, im Volksmund später die »Sächsische Bastille« genannt. Zahlreiche berühmte Gefangene saßen hier, in den kalten Arrestzellen, ihre Haftzeit ab: der Alchimist und Porzellan-Neuerfinder Johann Friedrich Böttger, August Bebel, Michail Bakunin, der Dichter Frank Wedekind und der Karikaturist Thomas Theodor Heine (wegen »Majestätsbeleidigung«).

Der letzte Kommandant verließ die Festung im Jahr 1913. Während des Ersten und Zweiten Weltkriegs wurden Kriegsgefangene auf die Festung gebracht. Meist handelte es sich dabei um französische, polnische und russische Generäle oder um andere hochrangige Offiziere.

Bei den schweren Luftangriffen auf die Stadt Dresden blieb die etwa 30 km entfernte Festung von Bomben verschont. Alle dort eingelagerten Kunstschätze und Dokumente überstanden den Zweiten Weltkrieg unbeschadet.

Mit Gründung der DDR wurde nach einer neuen Nutzung für die Festung Königstein gesucht. 1949 richtete der ostdeutsche Staat nach dem Vorbild sowjetisch-sta-

1. Blick über den Seigerturm auf die Festung mit Johann-Georgenburg, Streichwehr und Torhaus in unrenoviertem Zustand. In der Ferne (links im Bild) das Elbtal.

1. View over the Seiger Tower to the Fortress with Johann Georg Castle, Gatehouse and in the close-range defence in unrenovated condition. In the distance (left in the picture) the Elbe valley.

Introduction

Anyone who is interested in historic castles and fortresses in Europe will, sooner or later, come across the Königstein Fortress in Saxony. This is among the largest and most impressive buildings of its type. It is located not far from Dresden but in the middle of the Elbe sandstone mountains in Saxon Switzerland, making it a popular day trip destination for tourists, hikers, and climbers. Every year, half a million guests visit here – many of them families with children – to admire this noted attraction and, as the brochures say, to »conquer« it.

There are factual books on the history of the Fortress – in particular, *Festung Königstein* by Angelika Taube: a narrow volume, frequently reprinted, which contains the essential historical information and features plans and photographs, also serving as a travel guide. In 2017, a thick catalogue book on the new long-term exhibition written by the same author was published, with input by the Fortress curators and by numerous further specialists. We shall therefore restrict ourselves to the essential data.

Potsherd finds indicate that the rocky plateau located 247 m above the level of the Elbe and 361 m above sea level, which has a surface area of 9.5 ha, was a site of (temporary?) human occupation during the Bronze Age, 3000 years ago. The part of the castle and the fortress's history that we actually know of from documents and the remains of buildings began in the year 1241. This marks the first mention of the Königstein (»Lapis regis«) in documents. There was a burg on the rock plateau, whose remains are incorporated into the Johann Georg Castle of today. They form the primal cell or germ of the whole complex.

Initially, the castle of Königstein and the surrounding area belonged to Bohemia. In the year 1409, following the »Dohna Feud«, a shift in the power structure took place. The new owners were the Margraves of Meissen. Today, the border with Czech territory runs only a few kilometres up the Elbe, beyond Bad Schandau.

During the early period, the Königstein was primarily military, used to guard against and repel invasion. The position of the burg was optimal for this. From this vantage point, one could observe all the traffic along the Elbe and see any approaching hostile armies while they were still far off. Admittedly, the hills and the forested flat-topped mountains made the overview less than total. The valleys and trees offered sufficient cover to permit an unobserved approach. In spite of this, the massive sandstone walls inspired sufficient respect that the centuries that followed saw no major military attacks, sieges, or conflicts.

In the course of the 16th century, the Königstein had to be further developed to respond to the new firearms, which led to new ways of waging war. Not until the year 1589 could one call it a true fortress – more precisely, a »Landesfestung«, a »regional fortress«.

Providing for the needs of a constantly manned fortress required stores of provisions and a well, which was vital to survival.

This well was cut out of the rocks – or sunk, in mining terminology – between 1563 and 1569. It measures 152.5 m, making it one of the deepest wells in any European castle or fortress. It is a masterpiece of mining skill.

Due to the safety provided by the military and its fine location on the Elbe and in the Elbe sandstone mountains, the Saxon prince electors of the 17th century decided to also use the site as a centre for their passion for hunting. While they resided there, they hosted many eminent guests, and celebrated lavish feasts and carouses with wine, music, and dancing.

During the 17th and 18th century, this military fortress became a (elector) prince's pleasure palace. Admittedly, it did not have the luxury of a true pleasure palace, as

linistischer Umerziehungslager einen Jugendwerkhof ein. Das Projekt endete 1955.

Danach übernahm das DDR-Ministerium für Kultur die Festung. Das neue Ziel bestand darin, aus der touristisch so günstig gelegenen Anlage, inmitten des Elbsandsteingebirges, ein Museum zu machen.

Nach der Wende begannen, mit der Gründung des »Staatshochbauamtes«, des jetzigen »Staatsbetriebs Sächsisches Immobilien- und Baumanagement« (SIB) in Dresden, umfassende Sanierungsarbeiten. Jährlich stellt der Freistaat (oder das Land) Sachsen Millionen Euro für die Baumaßnahmen auf der Festung Königstein bereit. Auch das Landesamt für Denkmalpflege Sachsen wird eingeschaltet und achtet darauf, daß die historische Bausubstanz der Festung soweit wie möglich erhalten bleibt.

1991 übernahm Angelika Taube, die als Historikerin über einen der Staatsgefangenen auf der Festung promoviert hatte, die Geschäftsführung der Festung. Sie war damit Leiterin von mehr als 50 Beschäftigten, darunter wissenschaftliche Fachleute (Museologen und Historiker), ein Team für Öffentlichkeitsarbeit, Aufsichtspersonal, Kassiererinnen, Gärtner, technische sowie kaufmännische Angestellte und Reinigungspersonal.

Zu ihren Aufgaben gehörten auch – neben der Verwaltungstätigkeit – die Neukonzeption der bisher sehr kleinen, teilweise veralteten Ausstellungen und die Einrichtung einer größeren zentralen Dauerausstellung, in der die Geschichte von Burg und Festung für die neuen Besucherströme ausgebreitet werden sollte. Eine wichtige Entscheidung dabei war, daß alle bisher nur deutschsprachigen Erläuterungstexte in drei Sprachen zu verfassen und zu drucken waren: auf deutsch, englisch und tschechisch.

Mein Kontakt mit der Festung, die ich bisher nicht kannte, kam in den 1990er Jahren zustande. Ich hatte aus Dresden den Auftrag erhalten, ein Entwurfsgutachten für das veraltete und zu kleine Militärhistorische Museum der Bundeswehr – MHM (damals unter der Leitung von General von Prittwitz) zu entwickeln. Leider stießen meine Überlegungen auf keine Gegenliebe bei den Militärs. Die einzige Folge bestand darin, daß ein offener Architekturwettbewerb für Umbau und Neugestaltung des MHM in Dresden ausgeschrieben wurde. Bekanntlich ging Daniel Libeskind als Gewinner aus dem Verfahren hervor. Über seinen Entwurf mit dem gewagt-provozierenden Keil in Richtung der Dresdner Innenstadt gehen die Meinungen bis heute auseinander. Ich persönlich finde die realisierten Lösungen, obwohl sie

2. Luftansicht von Nordwesten, 2020.
3. Lageplan. 1 Torhaus, 2 Streichwehr, 3 Johann-Georgenburg 4 Neues Zeughaus, 5 Brunnenhaus, 6 Magdalenenburg, 7 Schatzhaus, 8 Altes Zeughaus.

2. Aerial view from the north-west, 2020.
3. Site plan. 1 Gatehouse, 2 close-range defence, 3 Johann Georg Castle, 4 New Armoury, 5 Well House, 6 Magdalena Castle, 7 Treasure House, 8 Old Armoury.

seen in Dresden, Moritzburg, or Pillnitz. A large banqueting hall/ballroom – today's New Armoury, formerly known as the »Johannis Hall« (completed 1631) – had suffice.

In the years between 1722 and 1725, August the Strong had coopers from Weimar, Durlach (today Karlsruhe) and Zweibrücken, a carpenter from Zurich and the Fortress's own cooper built a giant wine barrel in the cellar of the Magdalena Castle.

The external decorative architecture was designed by Matthäus Daniel Pöppelmann (1662–1736), at the time head master architect of the realm, who also built the Dresden Zwinger. The barrel can hold almost 240,000 litres of wine. The fun, however, did not last very long. The barrel was filled for the second time in 1740; a number of years later, in 1769, it showed the first signs of damage. In 1819, the giant wine barrel had to be broken up. Our art installation consisting of thousands of green wine bottles was created in 2010/11 in its memory, and to give an idea of how big the barrel would once have been. It has since received visitors from all over the world – who can view it on a special tour.

In the 18th and 19th century, the purpose for which the Fortress was used changed once again. As wars threatened, the official agencies of Royal Saxony, located in Dresden, had state funds, important documents, and artworks taken to the fortress to protect them from the enemy. In the 19th century, a dedicated, highly secure, vault-type »Schatzhaus« or »treasure house«, located near the Well House, was added to improve security. During the Second World War, the Fortress also served as a secure storage place for art.

As early as the late 16th century, individual fortress buildings were repurposed as feared state prisons (*Festungshaft*, »fortress custody«), causing the site to be popularly known as the »Saxon Bastille«. Numerous famous prisoners have served their time in the cold detention cells: the alchemist and reinventor of porcelain Johann Friedrich Böttger, August Bebel, Michail Bakunin, the poet Frank Wedekind, and the caricaturist Thomas Theodor Heine (for »*lèse-majesté*«).

The last commander departed the Fortress in 1913. During the First and Second World Wars, prisoners of war were brought to the Fortress. The majority of them were French, Polish, and Russian generals, or other high-ranking officers.

During the devastating air attacks on the city of Dresden, the Fortress, located around 30 km away, was

4. Die gewaltige Festungsmauer von Westen.

4. The massive fortress wall from the west.

wenig mit meinen Untersuchungen und Anregungen zu tun haben, sehr spannend und interessant.

Im Rahmen meiner Gutachtertätigkeit mußte ich auch die Dependance des MHM im Neuen Zeughaus und damit die Festung Königstein besuchen.

Als ich die 45 m hohe Felswand mit den Sandsteinmauern zum ersten Mal sah, war ich überwältigt. Ich konnte mich kaum satt sehen an diesem Meisterwerk von Natur-Architektur-Verschmelzung, die zwar im Ansatz bei allen Burgen und Festungen vorkommt, aber nirgendwo so harmonisch und gleichzeitig so mächtigabschreckend ausgeführt worden ist wie hier.

Daß ich in den nachfolgenden 25 Jahren etwa 200-mal hierherkommen würde, konnte ich damals nicht ahnen. Bei jedem Besuch, damit auch bei jedem Wetter, machte ich Photos von der mächtigen Sandsteinwand mit ihren Knickungen, Vor- und Rücksprüngen, Bastionen und Türmchen – bei Sonne, Regen, im Nebel und mit Schnee bedeckt.

Angelika Taube, die ich bei meinem ersten Besuch kennenlernte, war mit meinen bisherigen Arbeiten im Museums-, Ausstellungs- und Theaterbereich nicht vertraut.

Zum Gestaltungseinstieg lud sie mich ein, im großen Saal der Magdalenenburg eine Kunstinstallation einzurichten. Ich schlug eine fast raumgroße Spiegelfläche vor, waagrecht auf ein 50 cm hohes Podest gebaut. Besucher konnten das irritierende, auf dem Kopf stehende Raumbild, in dem sich die weißen Deckenwölbungen mit ihren markanten Kreuzgraten spiegelten, nur über einen schmalen Rundweg umgehen und bewundern. Sphärische Klänge aus Lautsprechern verstärkten die Impression, die zwischen Realität, Täuschung, Illusion und Fiktion schwebte.

Alle Reaktionen waren so begeistert, bei Publikum und Presse, daß einer jahrelangen Zusammenarbeit zwischen mir, der ich meinen Hauptwohnsitz mit Büro und Atelier in Süddeutschland habe, und der Festung nichts mehr im Wege stand.

In den letzten Jahren war es mir sogar möglich, eine Dauerausstellung im (frisch sanierten und renovierten) Neuen Zeughaus für das Militärhistorische Museum der Bundeswehr in Dresden zu entwerfen und zu realisieren.

Auf den nachfolgenden Seiten werden die wichtigsten Dauer- und Wechselausstellungen, die unter meiner künstlerischen Leitung auf der Festung zwischen 1998 und 2021 entstanden sind, dokumentiert. Chefkuratorin und Auftraggeberin blieb die ganzen Jahre über Angelika Taube. Sie wurde unterstützt von ihren Museologen Ingo Busse und Andrej Pawluschkow, eine Zeitlang auch von Susann Gutsche, später von den beiden Mittelalterhistorikern Markus Bitterlich und Maria Pretzschner (sie ist hauptsächlich zuständig für die Museumspädagogik), von ihren Assistentinnen Jenni Schwan und Katrin Harre, dem Graphikdesigner und Photographen Peter Mauksch und zahlreichen anderen, temporär mitarbeitenden Fachleuten. Am Ende des Buches werden sie alle noch einmal genannt.

Museums- und Ausstellungsprojekte sind immer Teamarbeiten. Zu diesem Team gehören natürlich auch – neben den ausführenden Firmen, den Medienfachleuten und Handwerkern – Architekten, die bei mir im Büro/Atelier tätig waren und sind: Melanie Brugger, Armin Teufel und Christin Seifert.

spared bombing. All of the art treasures and documents stored there survived the Second World War undamaged.

When the GDR was founded, a new use was sought for the Königstein Fortress. In 1949, the East German state set up a residential youth institution here modelled on Stalin-era Soviet re-education camps. The project ended in 1955.

The GDR's Ministry for Culture subsequently took over the Fortress. The new goal was to make this complex, so favourably situated for tourism purposes amid the Elbe sandstone mountains, into a museum.

Following the Reunification, and with the founding of the »Staatshochbauamt«, which is now the »Staatsbetrieb Sächsisches Immobilien- und Baumanagement« (SIB) in Dresden, extensive renovation work commenced. Annually, the Free State of Saxony makes millions of euros available for the construction work on the Königstein Fortress. The Landesamt für Denkmalpflege Sachsen (the regional authority for monument preservation for Saxony) is involved, and is responsible for ensuring that the Fortress's historic substance is preserved as far as possible.

In 1991, Angelika Taube, a historian who completed her Ph. D. on one of the state prisoners held at the Fortress, took on running it in business terms. This meant she was in charge of more than 50 people, including scientific experts (museologists and historians), a public outreach team, supervisory staff, cashiers, gardeners, technical and business personnel, and the cleaning staff.

In addition to administrative duties, her responsibilities included creating a new concept for the previously very small, partially outdated exhibitions and setting up a larger central long-term exhibition to present the history of the castle and Fortress to the new throng of visitors. One important decision that was taken was that all of the explanatory texts – previously German-language only – had to be written and printed in three languages: in German, English, and Czech.

My contact with the Fortress – previously unknown to me – took place in the 1990s. From Dresden, I received a commission to develop a draft report for the aged and too-small Bundeswehr Museum of Military History – MHM (then led by General von Prittwitz). Unfortunately, the military did not respond positively to my thoughts. The only consequence was that an open architecture competition for the conversion and redesign of the MHM in Dresden was held. As is well known, Daniel Libeskind emerged as the winner. To this day, opinions remain divided regarding his design: a daring and provocative wedge pointing in the direction of the Dresden inner city. Personally, I find the realised solutions very exciting and interesting, although they have little in common with my own investigations and inspirations.

In the course of my assessment, I also had to visit the branch of the MHM in the New Armoury, and therefore also the Königstein Fortress.

The first time I saw the rockface 45 m high with its sandstone walls, I was quite overwhelmed. I couldn't get enough of this masterful fusion of nature and architecture: something that exists to some extent for all castles and fortresses, but nowhere else is it so harmoniously and at the same time so powerfully and dauntingly executed as it is here.

At the time, I had no idea that, over the following 25 years, I would be coming here around 200 times. Every time I visited – in all weathers – I took photographs of the mighty sandstone rockface with its buckled places, its projections and recesses, its bastions and small towers – in the sun, in the rain, in the fog, and covered with snow.

On my first visit, I got to know Angelika Taube. She was not familiar with my previous work in the field of museums, exhibitions, and theatre.

As a way to begin my design work, she invited me to set up an art installation in the Magdalena Castle's great hall. I proposed a mirror surface taking up almost the full room, constructed horizontally on a 50 cm high pedestal. It offered a peculiar image of the space turned upside down, with a narrow walkway so that visitors can walk round it and admire it. It mirrors the white ceiling vaults, with their striking cross ridges. Spherical sounds from loudspeakers reinforce the impression that one is floating between reality, deception, illusion, and fiction.

The responses from the public and press were so unanimously enthusiastic that nothing stood in the way of a collaboration lasting years between me and the Fortress. My main residence, with my office and studio is located in South Germany.

Over the past years, it has even been possible for me to design and implement a long-term exhibition in the (newly renovated) New Armoury for the military history museum authorities in Dresden.

The following pages will document the most important long-term and short-term exhibitions that took place at the Fortress between 1998 and 2021, when I served as artistic director. Through all these years, Angelika Taube remained as chief curator and client. She was supported by her museologists, Ingo Busse and Andrej Pawluschkow, and also for a time by Susann Gutsche, and later by two historians of the medieval period, Markus Bitterlich and Maria Pretzschner (who is primarily responsible for the museum's educational programme), by her assistants Jenni Schwan and Katrin Harre, the graphic designer and photographer Peter Mauksch, and numerous other specialists working on a temporary basis. They are all named again at the end of the book.

Museum and exhibition projects are always a team effort. In addition to the firms who did the work, the media specialists and craftspeople, this team naturally also included the architects, past and present, who worked with me at my firm: Melanie Brugger, Armin Teufel and Christin Seifert.

»In lapide regis – Auf dem Stein des Königs. 800 Jahre Leben auf der Festung Königstein«, 2006–15

Dauerausstellung zur Geschichte des Königsteins im Torhaus und in der Streichwehr

Am 1. Mai 2015 wurde die neue Dauerausstellung »In lapide regis – Auf dem Stein des Königs« eröffnet. Obwohl nur von der regionalen Presse wahrgenommen und gewürdigt, kam sie bei den internationalen Besuchern – laut Besucherbuch und Interneteinträgen – sehr gut an. Bereits nach zwei Jahren konnte der 500 000. Besucher begrüßt werden.

Die Gesamtarbeit an dem Projekt, einschließlich Vorbesprechungen, Konzeptentwicklungen, Planungen, Bau von Modellen, Konstruktionszeichnungen, dauerte zehn Jahre. Als wir uns, die Ausstellungsplanergruppe, im Sommer 2006 auf der Festung zu den ersten Gesprächen im Büro von Angelika Taube trafen, wurde in der Dresdner Niederlassung I des SIB (Sächsisches Immobilien- und Baumanagement) noch über die Vorgehensweise und die Ziele der Sanierung und Modernisierung diskutiert. Ein Wettbewerbsverfahren folgte, aus dem das Berliner Büro Springer Architekten als Sieger hervorging.

Erst nach 2012 wurden die schadhaften historischen Holzdielenböden größtenteils herausgerissen, die alten Bodenfüllungen durch neue mit Dämmeigenschaften ersetzt, Fußboden- und Wandheizungen installiert, neue Dielen eingebaut, Sanitäranlagen geschaffen, Stromleitungen verlegt und moderne Beleuchtungskörper an den Gewölben und Wänden verteilt. (Lichtplanung: studio dinnebier, Berlin.) Für unseren Ausstellungseinbau blieb am Ende nur knapp ein Jahr übrig.

Insgesamt standen uns etwa 30 Räume mit 1200 m^2 Grundfläche, auf zwei Geschosse verteilt, zur Verfügung. Es war nicht einfach, die historischen Themen dramaturgisch einleuchtend in die teilweise seit Jahren leerstehenden, früher als Wohnungen benutzten, Räume einzufügen. Die zahlreichen Durchgänge, Fenster und Fensternischen, Rücksprünge und Pfeiler-Vorsprünge gaben den Rhythmus der Geschichtserzählung und der Einbauten vor.

Als wir nach dem üblichen Ausschreibungsverfahren eine Firma – es war die Heinzelmann GmbH aus Mühlacker – mit einem günstigen Angebot gefunden hatten und uns die 30 Räume schließlich in renoviertem Zustand übergeben wurden, mußten wir feststellen, daß kaum noch etwas wie früher aussah. Nur die Grundstrukturen der Räume und die Kreuzgrat-Gewölbedecken mit frischem, weißem Anstrich ließen noch etwas vom alten Festungscharakter erahnen. Der Ruinencharme, den ich persönlich so liebe, war leider gänzlich verschwunden, ebenso alle Spuren und Relikte aus der DDR-Zeit.

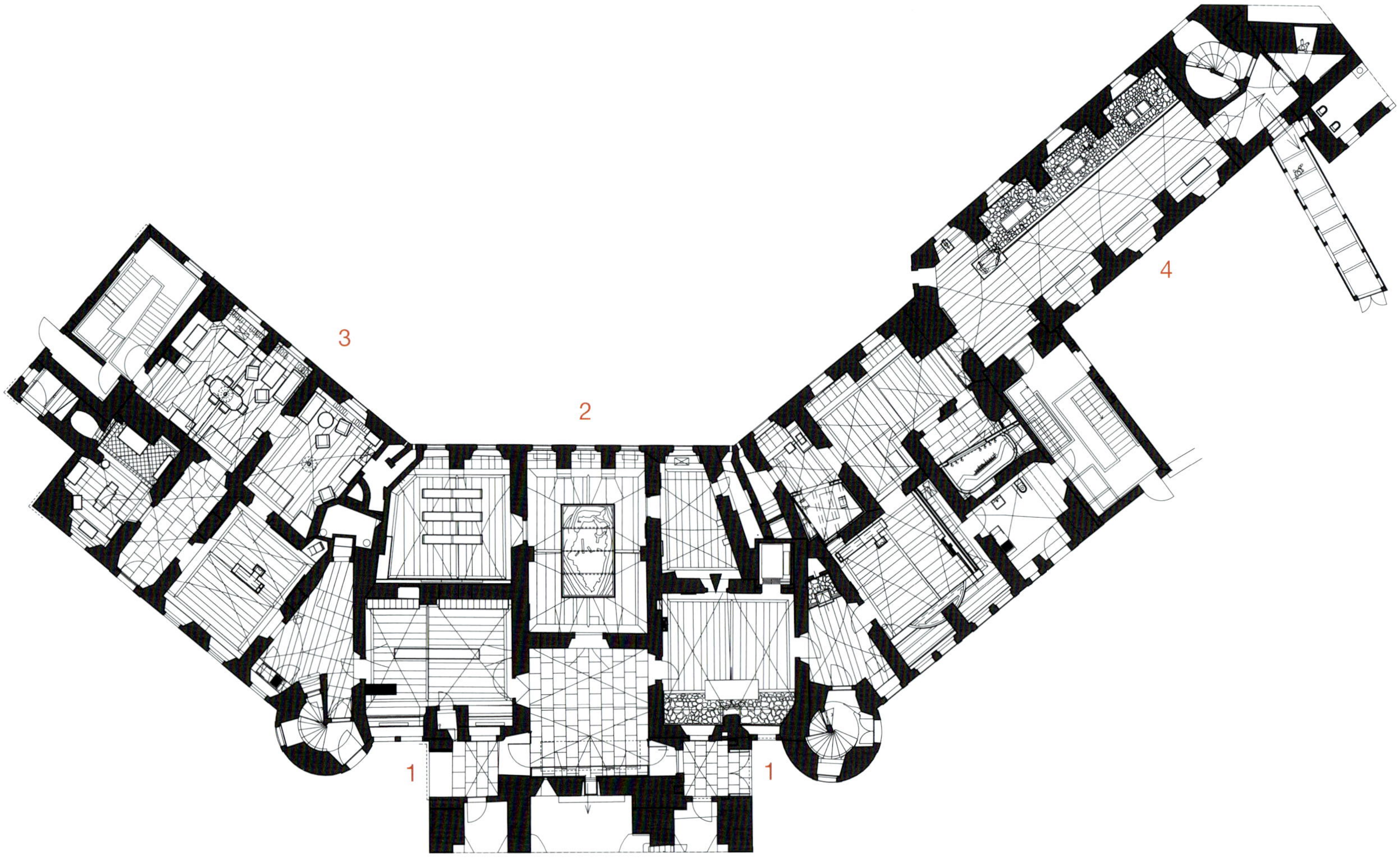

1. Der Ausstellungsrundgang beginnt in dem Raum mit der »Blauen Wand«.
2, 3. Grundrisse des Torhausbereichs (Erdgeschoß, Obergeschoß), in dem die Ausstellung eingerichtet wurde. 1 Eingang, 2 Torhaus, 3 Kommandantenwohnung, 4 Streichwehr.

1. The exhibition tour begins in the room with the »Blue Wall«.
2, 3. Floor plans of the Gatehouse area (ground floor, upper floor) where the exhibition was installed. 1 entrance, 2 Gatehouse, 3 commander's apartment, 4 close-range defence.

»In lapide regis – On the King's Stone. 800 Years of Life at the Königstein Fortress«, 2006–15
Long-term exhibition on the history of Königstein in the Gatehouse and in the close-range defence

The new long-term exhibition »In lapide regis – On the King's Stone« opened on the 1st of May 2015. Although it was recognised and covered only by the regional press, the visitor book and Internet response showed that it was well-received by international visitors. It welcomed its 500,000th visitor after just two years.

All the work on the project, including the preliminary discussions, concept development, planning, construction of models, and construction drawings, lasted ten years. When the members of the exhibition planning group met at the Fortress in Angelika Taube's office in the summer of 2006 for the first discussions, the Dresden branch I of the SIB (Sächsisches Immobilien- und Baumanagement) was still discussing the procedure and goals for the Fortress's renovation and modernisation. A competition process followed, with the Berlin firm of Springer Architekten emerging as the victor.

It was not until 2012 that the damaged historic wooden board floors were largely torn out, the old floor fills replaced with new ones with insulating properties, the floor and wall heating installed, new floorboards fitted, sanitary facilities provided, power cables laid, and modern illumination provided for the vaults and walls. (Lighting planning: studio dinnebier, Berlin.) This left us with just less than a year to install our exhibition.

In total, we had around 30 rooms with 1200 m^2 of floor space at our disposal, divided between two floors. It wasn't easy to incorporate the historic subject matter in a dramatic and illuminating way into rooms that had stood empty for years, and which, in some cases, had been used as housing. The numerous passageways, windows and window niches, recesses and pillared projections dictated the rhythm of the storytelling, and of the installations.

Having gone through the usual tendering process and found a firm offering a favourable estimate – Heinzelmann GmbH from Mühlacker – the 30 rooms were turned over to us in their new renovated condition, and we discovered that barely anything was the way it had been before. Only the basic structures of the rooms and the crossridge vaulted ceiling with its fresh white paint remains to suggest something of the old Fortress character. Unfortunately, the appeal of ruins – something that I personally love – was entirely gone, as were all traces and relics of the GDR period.

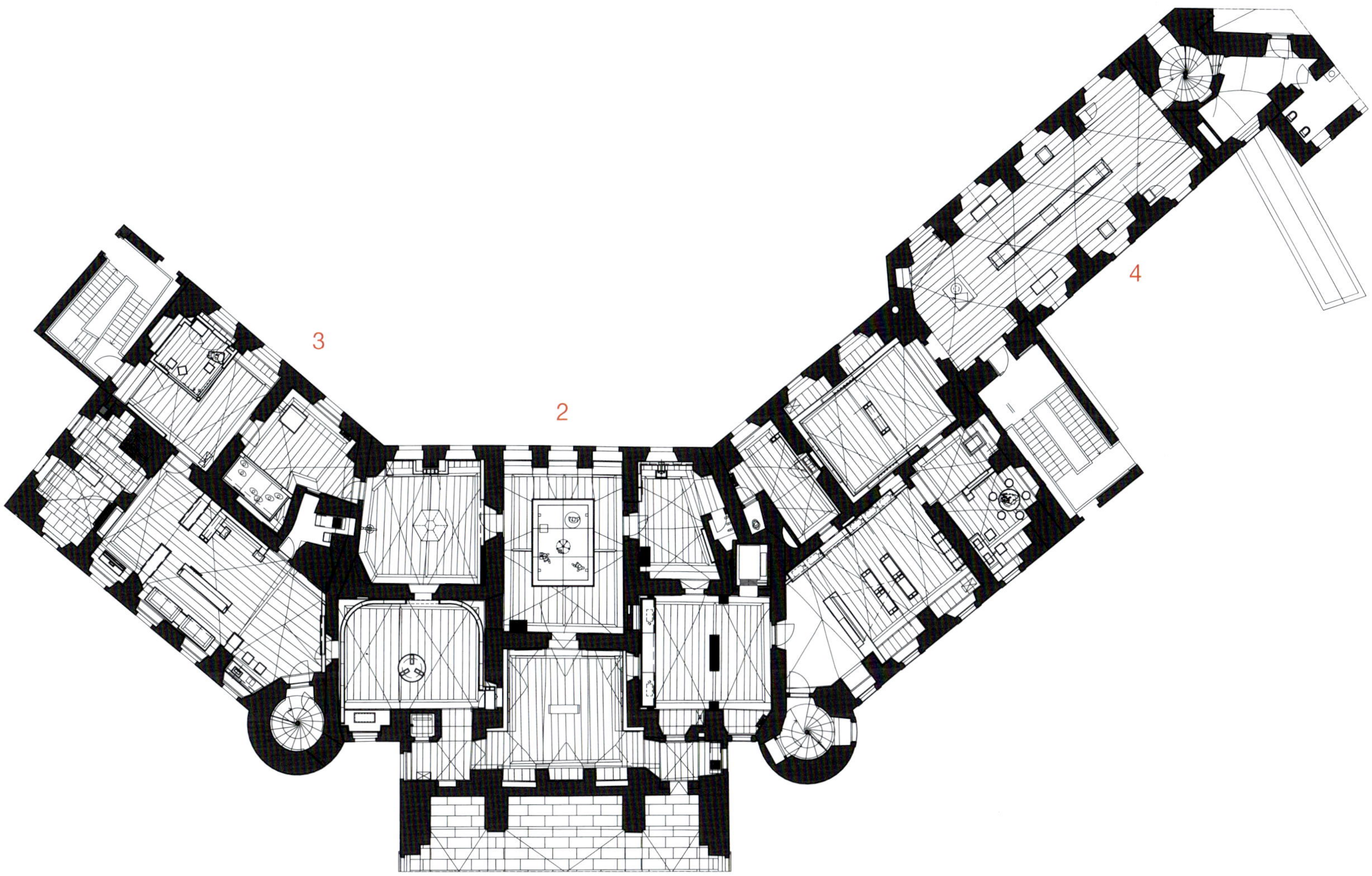

Bilder 3, 4

In diesem Raum wird die »Dohnaische Fehde« zu Beginn des 15. Jahrhunderts thematisiert. Der Fehde lag ein Streit zugrunde, der zwischen dem böhmischen König und den Wettiner Markgrafen in Meißen ausgebrochen war. Dabei kam es zum ersten Mal zur militärischen Belagerung des Königsteins. Erst nach vier Jahren gelang es den Truppen von Wilhelm I., den Königstein – einschließlich der umliegenden Ländereien und Dörfer – zu erobern und in die Mark Meißen einzugliedern. Danach ging der Königstein den Wettinern noch einmal verloren, und erst von 1409 an verblieb er ständig bei ihnen. 1459 wurden die neuen Besitzverhältnisse im Vertrag von Eger schriftlich fixiert.

Seither gilt der Wettiner Markgraf Wilhelm der Einäugige von Meißen (1343–1407) als eine wichtige regionale Siegerfigur. Sein Ganzkörper-Porträt auf der hinterleuchteten Stele vor einem Landschaftsphoto mit dem Königstein stammt von einem unbekannten Künstler, der es nach der Grabplatte im Dom zu Meißen (17. Jahrhundert) gezeichnet hat.

Links im Bild 4 eine Nachbildung der ehemaligen Klosterpforte. 1516 wurde auf dem Festungsplateau ein Cölestinerkloster mit zwölf Mönchen gegründet. Es existierte nur acht Jahre lang und löste sich unter dem Einfluß der Reformation wieder auf.

Bild 1

Die »Blaue Wand« konnte von den Restauratoren gerettet werden und dient nun als Ausstellungsfläche mit zwei kleinen Wandvitrinen, in denen ein Sandstein mit einem Muschelabdruck aus der Kreidezeit und bronzezeitliche Scherbenfunde ausgestellt werden, die vor einigen Jahren bei Bauarbeiten auf der Festung ans Tageslicht kamen. Der Muschelabdruck beweist das Vorhandensein eines Meeres anstelle des Gebirges vor Jahrmillionen, die Scherben beweisen, daß das Festungsplateau schon vor über 3000 Jahren, zumindest temporär, besiedelt war.

Bild 2

Die ersten Ausstellungsräume im Erdgeschoß stehen unter dem Titel »Von der Entstehung des Königsteins bis zur mittelalterlichen Burg«. Sie erhielten alle zunächst dunkle, dann langsam heller werdende Wand- und Deckenanstriche. Außerdem wurden zwei Sockelbereiche in Richtung der Außenwände mit Feldern aus Sandsteinbrocken belegt. Sie sollen an das Baumaterial der mittelalterlichen Burg erinnern.

Picture 1
The »Blue Wall« was saved by the restorers, and now serves as a display surface with two small wall-mounted cases displaying a shell impression from the Cretaceous Age and Bronze Age pottery fragments, which came to light a number of years ago during construction work on the Fortress. The shell impressions prove that a sea existed where the rock is now millions of years ago, while the fragments prove that the Fortress's plateau was inhabited, at least temporarily, more than 3000 years ago.

Picture 2
The first exhibition rooms on the ground floor are entitled »Von der Entstehung des Königsteins bis zur mittelalterlichen Burg« (»The Königstein: From its Birth to the Mediaeval Castle«). Their walls and ceilings were all painted in dark tones that gradually lighten. Additionally, two foundation areas in the direction of the outer walls were laid with sections of broken sandstone rock. These are meant as a reminder of the construction materials of the mediaeval castle.

Pictures 3, 4
The subject of this room is the »Dohna Feud« of the early 15th century. This feud was the cause of a conflict between the King of Bohemia and the Margrave of Wettin, the sovereign of the Mark of Meissen. This led to the first military siege of the Königstein. It took four years for the troops of Wilhelm I to conquer the Königstein – together with the surrounding lands and villages – and incorporate the whole into the Mark of Meissen. The Wettiners subsequently lost the Königstein, and it was not until 1409 that they regained it permanently. In 1459, the new ownership was finalised in the Treaty of Eger.

This established Wettin's Margrave Wilhelm the One-Eyed of Meissen (1343–1407) as an important victorious regional figure. The full-figure portrait of him shown on a backlit stele in front of a landscape photo featuring the Königstein is by an unknown artist who drew it based on his tomb in the cathedral of Meissen (17th century).

In the picture 4 on the left: a replica of the former monastery gate. In 1516, a Celestine monastery was founded on the Fortress plateau, home to twelve monks. It existed for only eight years, with the Reformation leading to its dissolution.

Bild 5
Auf dem Photo ist ein Raumausschnitt mit einer nachgestellten, fiktiven Gesprächsszene zwischen dem italienischen Architekten und einem kursächsischen Beamten zu sehen. (Körper, Gesicht und Hände von Lisa Büscher, Kostüme von Alexandra Hahn, dazu Toninstallation, geschrieben von Markus Bitterlich.)

Bild 6
Mit dem großen, neu gebauten Diorama (von Paul Wells) erhalten die Besucher einen stimmungsvollen Eindruck von der Festungsbaustelle in den Jahren zwischen 1589 und 1592. Zeitweise arbeiteten hier über 500 Personen: Bergleute, Steinbrecher, Steinspitzer, Steinmetzen, Maurer, Zimmerleute, Schieferdecker, Schmiede und Tischler sowie zahlreiche Fronarbeiter. Das Baumaterial stammte aus der Umgebung: der Sandstein aus den Felsen vom Königstein, das Holz aus den Wäldern ringsum.

Man erkennt hinter der großen Festungsmauer die zeitgleich errichteten Kasematten.

Zur Irritation wurde zwischen die Handwerker des 16. Jahrhunderts auch eine heutige Bauarbeiterfigur postiert, die zum Programm der interaktiven Museumspädagogik gehört, entwickelt von Maria Pretzschner. Die große Dioramavitrine steht in einem fensterlosen, schwarz angestrichenen Raum, angrenzend an den Museumsrundweg. Der Raum war früher als Küche benutzt worden.

Bild 7
Blick in den letzten, langgezogenen Erdgeschoßraum, die »Streichwehr«, die früher im Kellergeschoß mit Kanonen bestückt war. Mit den beiden vorherigen Räumen steht sie unter dem Titel »Ausbau zur Landesfestung und Dreißigjähriger Krieg (16. und 17. Jahrhundert)«.

Picture 5
The photo shows a section of the space with a recreated fictional scene of discussion between the Italian architect and an official of the Electorate of Saxony. (Body, face, and hands by Lisa Büscher, costumes by Alexandra Hahn, sound installation written by Markus Bitterlich.)

Picture 6
The newly-constructed large diorama (by Paul Wells) gives visitors an atmospheric impression of the Fortress building site in the years between 1589 and 1592. At times, there were more than 500 people working here: miners, stone-breakers, stone pointers, stonemasons, bricklayers, joiners, roof slaters, smiths and carpenters, and numerous serfs. The construction materials were taken from the surrounding area: sandstone from the rocks of the Königstein, wood from the surrounding forests.

Behind the big Fortress wall, one can see the casemates that were erected at the same time.

As an interesting disruption, a figure of a modern day construction worker is positioned between the 16th century labourers. This figure is part of the interactive museum education program developed by Maria Pretzschner.

The large diorama glass case stands in a windowless side room with the walls painted black, adjoining the museum concourse. This room was previously used as a kitchen.

Picture 7
A view of the final room on the ground storey, which is elongated. This is the »close-range defence«, previously stocked with cannons in the cellar storey. It is grouped with the two previous rooms under the title »Expansion to a Regional Fortress and the Thirty Years' War (16th and 17th centuries)«.

Bild 8
Im Obergeschoß angekommen: Blick in den langgezogenen Ausstellungsraum (obere Streichwehr), der mit seinen renovierten weißen Gewölben, dem neuen Holzfußboden und der neuen Beleuchtung (studio dinnebier) dem unteren Streichwehrraum aufs Haar gleicht.

Die historischen Themen im ersten Obergeschoß lauten: »Augusteisches Zeitalter«, »Die Königszimmer«, »Von Napoleon bis zum Sperrfort des Deutschen Reiches«, »Vom 1. Weltkrieg bis zur Eröffnung des Museums«.

Bilder 9, 10
Im Zentrum des Raumes steht eine schmale, lange Vitrine, in der ein königlicher Kutschenzug nachgebildet wurde. (Wagen und Landschaft von Paul Wells, Figuren und Pferde von Sarah Hendry, beide England.) Der genaue Titel lautet: »August der Starke reist mit seinem Hofstaat auf die Festung Königstein«.

Die Festung Königstein wurde von den sächsischen Kurfürsten, die zeitweise auch Könige von Polen waren, nicht nur als eine rein militärische Anlage betrachtet, sondern auch als Ort der Feste. Ein Ziel des reisenden Hofstaats war – innerhalb unserer Rauminszenierung so dargestellt – das »Große Weinfaß«, das Matthäus Daniel Pöppelmann mit reichem Holzschmuck, mit Pokalen und einer Bacchusfigur verziert hatte.

Vor den Fenstern auf beiden Seiten stehen in den Raumnischen links und rechts des Kutschenzugs vier große Vitrinen. Darin ausgestellt sind auf Glasböden Teller, Gläser, Kaffeekannen, Teedosen, Tassen, Bestecke, Tabletts, Leuchter, Pokale, Humpen, Medaillen, Schatullen und Koffer aus dem 18. Jahrhundert. Zwei Gipsabgüsse von historischen Büsten stehen, auf weißen Sockelsäulen, in den beiden mittleren Fensternischen. Dabei handelt es sich um die Porträts von König August II. von Polen, Kurfürst von Sachsen, genannt August der Starke (Originalbüste von Paul Heermann, 1718) und von Kronprinz Friedrich August von Sachsen (das Original stammt von François Coudray, 1714/15).

Picture 8
Arriving in the upper storey: a view of the long exhibition room (upper close-range defence), which, with its renovated white vaults, the new wood flooring and the new illumination (studio dinnebier), is identical to the lower close-range defence space.

The historic themes of the first upper storey are: »The Augustan Age«, »The King's Rooms«, »From Napoleon to the Stronghold of the German Empire«, »From the 1st World War to the Museum Opening.«

Pictures 9, 10
In the centre of the space is a long narrow glass case containing a replica of a royal carriage procession. (Coach and landscape by Paul Wells, figures and horses by Sarah Hendry, both from England.) The precise title is: »August the Strong travels with his court to the Königstein Fortress«.

The Saxon Prince Electors – who were at times also Kings of Poland – regarded the Königstein Fortress as more than a purely military complex: it was also a place of festivities. A destination of the travelling court was – as presented in our staged space – the »great wine barrel«, decorated by Matthäus Daniel Pöppelmann with elaborate wood ornamentation, with goblets, and with a figure of Bacchus.

In front of the windows on both sides, in the room niches to the left and right of the carriage procession, are four large glass cases. Displayed inside on glass are plates, glasses, coffee pots, tea caddies, cups, cutlery, saucers, lamps, goblets, tankards, medals, caskets, and cases from the 18th century. Two plaster casts from historical busts, on white pillar pedestals, are standing in the two central window niches. These are the portraits of King August II of Poland, Prince Elector of Saxony, known as August the Strong (original bust by Paul Heermann, 1718) and Crown Prince Friedrich August of Saxony (original created by François Coudray, 1714/15).

Bilder 11, 12

Der Venezianer Bernardo Bellotto (Canaletto, 1722–1780; nicht zu verwechseln mit seinem Onkel Giovanni Antonio Canal, der ebenso unter dem Namen Canaletto bekannt war) malte in seiner faszinierenden, nahezu photorealistischen Manier (und das inmitten der Barockzeit!) im Auftrag des sächsischen Kurfürsten und Königs August III. in den Jahren 1756 bis 1758 fünf Bilder der Festung Königstein: drei Außenansichten und zwei Innenansichten mit Szenen des Alltagslebens. Da zur gleichen Zeit der Siebenjährige Krieg ausbrach und sein königlicher Auftraggeber mit dem gesamten Hofstaat und der Staatskasse nach Warschau floh, sah sich Canaletto gezwungen, alle seine Königstein-Gemälde an einen englischen Kunsthändler zu verkaufen. Zwei davon befinden sich heute im Besitz der Manchester City Galleries. Das dritte Gemälde hängt in der National Gallery of Art in Washington DC. Die zwei »englischen« Darstellungen der Festung Königstein kehrten bisher nur einmal nach Deutschland zurück. Sie wurden 2014 bei einer Sonderausstellung (mit Katalogbuch) unter dem Titel »Die Schönste im ganzen Land – Die Festung im Spiegel der Kunst« in der Magdalenenburg auf dem Königstein gezeigt.

Im Zentrum unseres Canaletto-Raumes »hängt« – als hinterleuchtetes Dia – die Ansicht der Festung von Westen. Fast alle Hügel ringsum sind unbewaldet, bis auf die Nordseite, den steilen Berghang hinunter zur Elbe. Die offen-freie, abgeholzte Hügellandschaft wird von wenigen Wegen durchzogen. Einer davon führt hinauf zum Festungshaupteingang. Im Vordergrund des Gemäldes sieht man weidende Kühe, begleitet von Mägden und Hirten.

Die Festung selbst wirkt wie ein Bergschloß, das auf einem mächtigen Sandsteinblock erbaut wurde. Von den Gebäuden sind vor allem die Johann-Georgenburg, die Streichwehr und das Torhaus zu sehen. Für den militärischen Trutz-Aspekt schien sich Canaletto nicht sonderlich zu interessieren.

Auf den beiden anderen Gemälden von Canaletto, die ebenfalls als hinterleuchtete Dias in Originalgröße gezeigt werden, sieht man alltägliche Szenen auf dem sommerlich gestimmten Festungsplateau, Platzbereiche vor der Magdalenenburg und hinter dem Brunnenhaus. Licht und Schatten beleben die Architekturen, Mauern, Zäune und Menschen. Körper und Räume werden sichtbar. Fernblicke werden nur in schmalen Häuserlücken angedeutet. Der weite Himmelshorizont, von wenigen Wolken (ohne Vögel) durchzogen, muß genügen.

Die Titel der zwei Gemälde lauten: *Kommandantengarten und Brunnenhaus auf der Festung Königstein* (links) und *Magdalenenburg, Brunnenhaus und Johannissaal* (rechts).

Erstaunlich, wie genau Canaletto hinschaute und mit Hilfe der Camera obscura die Realität nahezu unverzerrt und ungeschönt (nehmen wir an) malte. Er interessierte sich weder für die Götter noch für mythologische Allegorien, eher für den Alltag, die Menschen, das Licht und den Raum.

An allen Hausfassaden (vor allem an der Magdalenenburg) zeigt er Verletzungen und Beschädigungen in den Putzbereichen. Er scheint sich für feuchte Stellen, herunterlaufendes Wasser, Risse und Abbruchstellen geradezu zu begeistern. Alle Architekturen wirken mit dieser Patina so malerisch gealtert wie in seiner Heimatstadt Venedig. Leider fehlten ihm hier, auf der Festung Königstein, die spiegelnden Wasserflächen, wie sie seine berühmten Ansichten von Pirna und Dresden mit dem Wasser der Elbe zeigen.

Dafür beschäftigte sich Canaletto ausführlich mit den Menschen, die er (wahrscheinlich) auf der Festung antraf. Er liebte bunte Gesellschaftsquerschnitte. Ein Gemisch aus Handwerkern, Soldaten, höheren Militärs, Invaliden, vornehmen Adligen mit ihren Dienern, ersten Touristen und fleißigen, Wäsche aufhängenden oder im Garten arbeitenden Hausfrauen, die manchmal arrogant dahinstelzenden adligen Damen, von Kavalieren begleitet, begegnen. Kutschen und Marktstände wie auf den Plätzen in Dresden und Pirna gab es hier oben auf der Festung nicht.

Von heute aus gesehen, haben die Gemälde Ähnlichkeit mit vergrößerten Dokumentarphotos (Dias). Momentaufnahmen (stills) eines normalen Sommertags, eingefangen wie ein authentisches Zeitbild, ohne jede Überhöhung, Verklärung oder sonstige Verzerrung der Realität. Mag sein, daß er die Zeitpunkte mancher Begegnungen zeitlich gerafft hat. Tatsache ist (bei ihm immer): Es herrscht eine friedliche, fast träge Ruhe. Die Tätigkeiten scheinen sehr langsam zu geschehen (so macht es den Eindruck). Oder sind alle Figuren für einen Moment – für die Ewigkeit? – erstarrt, aus der Zeit gekippt?

Man zeigte sich öffentlich, man verbarg weder Faulheit noch Langeweile und schien sich eine gewisse Neugier bewahrt zu haben. Kaum vorzustellen, daß sich gleichzeitig ringsum ein Krieg zusammenbraute, daß Sachsen bald von preußischen Soldaten besetzt und daß in den nächsten Jahren Canalettos Haus in Dresden, einschließlich vieler seiner Gemälde, durch Kanonenbeschuß (Bombardierungen) zerstört werden würde.

Die Originalgemälde von Canalettos 14 berühmten Ansichten Dresdens hängen heute in der Galerie Alter Meister beim Zwinger, auch seine Ansichten von Pirna.

multiple meeting situations. In point of fact, a peaceful and almost languid calm predominates, as is always the case with Canaletto. Their actions appear to be taking place very slowly (at least, that is the impression that we have). Or are all the figures frozen for a moment – for eternity? Are they caught out of time?

People show themselves openly, not concealing idleness or boredom; they seemed to have preserved a certain curiosity. It is hard to believe that, at the very same time, a war is already looming on all sides; that Saxony will soon be occupied by Prussian soldiers, and that, in the next few years, Canaletto's house in Dresden, along with a number of his paintings, would be destroyed by cannon fire in a bombardment.

The original painting of Canaletto's 14 famous views of Dresden hangs today in the of Old Masters at the Zwinger, with his views of Pirna.

Pictures 11, 12

In the years between 1756 and 1758, the Venetian artist Bernardo Bellotto (Canaletto, 1722–1780; not to be confused with his uncle Giovanni Antonio Canal also known as Canaletto) was commissioned by the Saxon Prince Elector and King August III to paint five pictures – all in his fascinating, almost photorealistic manner (and during the Baroque period, at that!) – of the Königstein Fortress: three exterior views, and two interior views with scenes from everyday life. Because the Seven Years' War broke out at this time, causing his royal client to flee to Warsaw along with his whole court and the royal coffers, Canaletto felt compelled to sell all his Königstein paintings to an English art dealer. Two of them are today in the possession of the Manchester City Galleries. The third painting hangs in the National Gallery of Art in Washington DC. The two »English« Königstein Fortress pictures have hitherto returned to Germany only once. In 2014, they were shown in a special exhibition entitled »The Fairest in the Country. Königstein Fortress in the Mirror of Art« in the Magdalena Castle at the Königstein.

In the centre of the Canaletto room »hangs« the view of the Fortress from the west (it is in fact a backlit transparency). Almost all the hills around it are unforested, except for the north side, the steep slope down to the Elbe. This open, deforested hilly landscape has a few roads running through it. One of them leads up to the Fortress's main entrance. In the painting's foreground, we can see grazing cows, accompanied by maids and shepherds.

The Fortress itself appears like a castle fortress constructed on a mighty sandstone block. Out of the buildings, only the Johann Georg Castle, the close-range defence, and the Gatehouse can be seen. Canaletto does not appear to have been especially interested in the aspect of military defence.

In the other two pictures by Canaletto – which are also displayed as backlit transparencies in their original size – we see everyday scenes from the Fortress plateau (with a summer ambience), areas in front of the Magdalena Castle and behind the Well House. Light and shadows bring to life the architecture, the walls, the fences, and the people. Bodies and spaces are visible. More distant prospects can be seen only through narrow gaps between the buildings. The wide sky of the horizon, with a few clouds (no birds) must suffice.

The titles of the two paintings are: *Commander's Garden and Well House at the Königstein Fortress*, left, and *Magdalena Castle, Well House and Johannis Hall*, right.

It is astonishing just how precise Canaletto's gaze was and how he painted reality in an almost undistorted and unembellished way (at least, so we assume) with the aid of the camera obscura. He is not interested in gods or in mythological allegories, but in everyday life, in people, in light, and in space.

He shows damage and wear to the plasterwork on the façades of all the buildings (especially the Magdalena Castle), and seems to have a positive enthusiasm for spots of damp, dripping water, cracks, and broken places. With this patina, all of the pieces of architecture look as artistically aged as in his home city of Venice. Unfortunately, the Königstein Fortress does not offer the reflective expanses of water that appear in his famous views of Pirna and Dresden (where the Elbe supplies water surfaces).

Instead, Canaletto gives extensive attention to the people, who are (probably) people he met at the Fortress. He loved a colourful cross-section of society. A mix of labourers, soldiers, high-ranking military figures, invalids, elegant aristocrats with their servants, early tourists, housewives diligently hanging out washing or working in the garden, and noble ladies pacing in a sometimes arrogant manner, accompanied by cavaliers. Here at the Fortress, there are no coaches and market stands of the kind seen in squares in Dresden and Pirna.

Seen from today's perspective, the paintings bear a similarity to enlarged documentary photos (transparencies). These are still-image snapshots of a normal summer's day, captured like authentic images of the time, with no exaggeration, false glamour or other distortions of reality. It may be that he has created a timelapse of

Bild 13

Im Vorraum zu unserer Spiegelpodest-Inszenierung hängen an den Wänden sechs große Porträt-Gemälde. Im Zentrum, links und rechts von der Durchgangstür: König August II. von Polen, Kurfürst von Sachsen, genannt August der Starke, gemalt von einem unbekannten Künstler nach einem Gemälde von Louis de Silvestre (Professor an der Dresdner Kunstakademie), nach 1723.

Daneben Christiane Eberhardine von Brandenburg-Bayreuth, Gemahlin von August II., gemalt nach einem Originalbild von Louis de Silvestre, nach 1720. An den Wänden links und rechts befinden sich jeweils zwei Gemälde von sächsischen Generälen, die zur damaligen Zeit – wegen ihrer siegreichen Beteiligung am Krieg gegen die Türken vor Wien – als Helden verehrt wurden.

Bild 14

Im ehemaligen Speisesaal der »Königszimmer« wurden drei historische Figuren (Körper, Arme, Hände, Beine, Füße, Köpfe mit Gesichtern von Lisa Büscher, Kostüme von Alexandra Hahn) in Lebensgröße nachgebildet. Es handelt sich (links) um König August II. von Polen, hier als Friedrich August I., Kurfürst von Sachsen, genannt August der Starke, im Alter von 58 Jahren und König Friedrich Wilhelm I. von Preußen (rechts) im Alter von 40 Jahren (später Soldatenkönig genannt), dazwischen Gräfin Anna Karolina Orzelska, illegitime Tochter Augusts des Starken im Alter von 21 Jahren.

Sie treffen hier (fiktiv) im Januar 1728 aufeinander, um in den nächsten Momenten den Johannis- oder Heldensaal – heute: Neues Zeughaus – zu betreten. Dort wurde für sie und die übrigen Gäste von Dienern eine lange Speisetafel mit weißen Tischdecken aus Damast, königlichem Porzellan und Silberbesteck, mit duftendem Braten (Wild aus den Wäldern ringsum), Gemüse und Wein angerichtet.

Das Spiegelpodest soll, einschließlich des rekonstruierten Kronleuchters (Firma Christoph Palme) an der Decke und der Musik von Johann Friedrich Fasch, auf den einstigen Glanz des sächsischen Hofes, auch bei königlichen Festen auf dem Königstein, hinweisen: eine Imagination zwischen Geschichtsvergegenwärtigung, Wachsfigurenkabinett und möglicher historischer Wahrheit.

Bild 15

Raum mit einem von uns leicht vergrößerten Panorama der Festung. Die Vorzeichnungen der einzelnen Bilder stammen von Leopold Ludwig von Schirnding, der zwischen 1827 und 1831 auf der Festung als »Sous lieutenant« diente. In den Jahren danach gab er seine Vorlagen an den Dresdner Drucker Karl Wilhelm Arldt weiter, der daraus Lithographien herstellte und diese 1847 als Loseblattsammlung in einer Mappe herausgab.

In unserem Ausstellungsraum wurden die malerischen Ausblicke auf das Elbsandsteingebirge und die Elbe mit zahlreichen historisch-authentischen Garten-, Terrassen-, Mauer- und Felsansichten der Festung (besser: angeschnittene Fragmente davon) auf Folien und Acrylglas gedruckt. Um die Wirkung zu steigern, erhielten sie Kunstlicht von hinten (und werden zu Dias).

An den dargestellten Menschen mit ihren Kleidern und Frisuren erkennt man die Biedermeierzeit. Moden haben kurze »Lebensphasen«. Landschaft, Naturelemente und Himmel sind immer gleich, sie ändern ihre Erscheinungsformen kaum – trotz späterer verkehrstechnischer und architektonischer Eingriffe.

Picture 13
On the walls of the anteroom to our mirror platform presentation, six large portraits are hanging. In the centre, to the left and right of the connecting door: King August II of Poland, Prince Elector of Saxony (known as August the Strong), painted by an unknown artist based on a painting by Louis de Silvestre (a professor at the Dresden Kunstakademie), after 1723.

Beside it is Christiane Eberhardine von Brandenburg-Bayreuth, the consort of August II, painted based on an original painting by Louis de Silvestre, after 1720. On the walls to the left and right, there are two paintings of Saxon generals, who were honoured as heroes at the time because of their victories in the war against the Turks near Vienna.

Picture 14
In the former dining room of the »King's Rooms«, three life-sized historic figures (bodies, arms, hands, legs, feet, heads, and faces by Lisa Büscher, costumes by Alexandra Hahn) are depicted. They are: (on the left) King August II of Poland, here as Friedrich August I, Prince Elector of Saxony, known as August the Strong, at the age of 58 years, (to the right) King Friedrich Wilhelm I of Prussia, aged 40 years (later known as the Soldier King), and (between them) the Countess Anna Karolina Orzelska, illegitimate daughter of August the Strong, aged 21 years.

They meet here (fictionally) in January 1728, and, in the next few moments, they enter the Johannis Hall or Heroes Hall, which is the New Armoury of today. There, a long table was being artfully decked out by servants with a white damask tablecloth, royal porcelain and silver cutlery, with fragrant roasts (game from the surrounding forests), vegetables, and wine for them and for all the other guests.

The mirror platform – including the reconstructed chandelier on the ceiling by the firm of Christoph Palme and the music by Johann Friedrich Fasch – is intended as a reminder of the former glory of the Saxon court, as seen in royal feasts at the Königstein: a work of imagination lying somewhere between bringing the past to life, a chamber of waxworks, and a possible historical truth.

Picture 15
Room with a panorama of the Fortress, slightly enlarged by us. The preliminary drawings for the individual pictures were by Leopold Ludwig von Schirnding, who served as a »sous lieutenant« at the Fortress between 1827 and 1831. In the years that followed, he gave his drafts to the Dresden printer Karl Wilhelm Arldt, who produced lithographs from them and issued them in 1847 as a loose-leaf collection in a folder.

In our exhibition space, the picturesque views of the Elbe sandstone mountains and the Elbe, with numerous historically authentic views of the gardens, terraces, walls, and rocks of the Fortress (or rather: fragments or details of them) are printed on film and acrylic glass. In order to heighten the effect, they are backlit with artificial light (making them transparencies).

The clothes and hairstyles of the people represented here show that they are of the Biedermeier era. Fashions have a short »lifespan«. The landscape, natural elements, and sky are always the same, barely altering their appearance – in spite of subsequent transport-related and architectonic interventions.

Bild 16
Raum mit einer zentralen Vitrine, in der sich Waffen aus dem 19. Jahrhundert befinden. An der rechten Wand Scherenschnitte des Leipziger Künstlers Steve Viezens. Sein vorgegebenes Thema: das »Königsteinlied« mit der Nennung diverser Handwerksberufe, die auf der Festung vertreten waren. Das Lied selbst kann in einer Hörstation auf der Bank am Fenster angeklickt und gehört werden.

Bild 17
Der Raum mit den von Restauratoren freigelegten gelben Wänden. In einer großen Vitrine sind vor dem Porträt König Alberts von Sachsen (1828–1902) Militaria – Uniformen, Säbel, Gewehre, Granatkörbe, Helme und Mützen – aus dem späten 19. Jahrhundert ausgestellt: Bilder einer Zeit, in der das Militär noch zur repräsentativen Gesellschaftsschicht gehörte. Soldaten und Offiziere bereicherten mit ihren bunten Uniformen die Alltagsbilder der Festung, der Dorf- und Stadtstraßen, der Cafés und Restaurants.

Bild 18
Große Raum-Vitrine mit der Rekonstruktion einer Gefangenenstube aus der Zeit des Ersten Weltkriegs. Im Vordergrund ein Photograph, der seinen Kopf und seinen Oberkörper – wie damals üblich – unter einem großen Tuch versteckt. Sein fertiges, hinterleuchtetes Photo ist auf der gegenüberliegenden Wandseite zu sehen: russische Offiziere als Kriegsgefangene auf der Festung Königstein, um einen Tisch versammelt. Sie lesen Zeitung, trinken Tee und essen Kuchen.

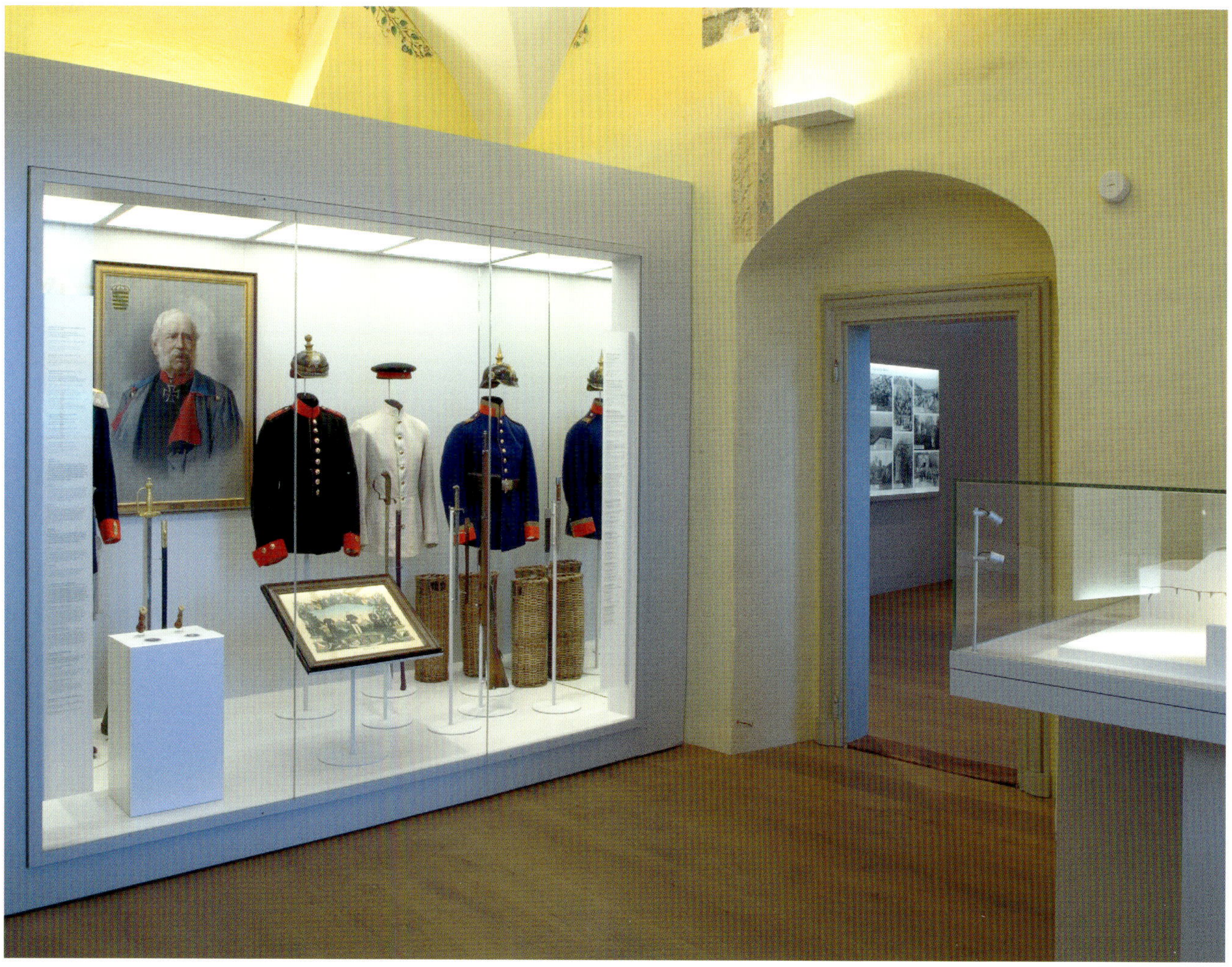

Picture 16
Room with a central glass case, containing 19th century weapons. On the right-hand wall are cut-out silhouettes by the Leipzig artist Steve Viezens. He was given as his theme the »Königsteinlied«, with its naming of various forms of manual craftwork that would have occurred at the Fortress. The song itself can be heard – with a single click – at a listening station at the bench by the window.

Picture 17
The room with the yellow walls, as revealed by the restorers. A large glass case contains the portrait of King Albert of Saxony (1828–1902). Arranged in front of the portrait are items of militaria from the late 19th century – uniforms, sabres, arms, grenade baskets, helmets, and caps. These are images from a time when the military still belonged to a prestigious class of society. Soldiers and officers in their bright uniforms added colour to the day-to-day life of the Fortress, the streets of the village and town, and the cafés and restaurants.

Picture 18
A large glass case, filling the room, with a reconstruction of a prisoner's cell from the First World War era. In the foreground is a photographer – as was usual during this era, he has his head and upper body concealed beneath a large cloth. His completed photo can be seen on the opposite wall (backlit): Russian officers, who were prisoners of war at the Königstein Fortress, gathered around a table. They are reading newspapers, drinking tea, and eating cake.

Altes Zeughaus, 2018–20

Als Ergänzung zu unserer Dauerausstellung im Torhaus und in der Streichwehr, in der die politische, gesellschaftliche und architektonische Geschichte der Festung erzählt wird, hier die Fokussierung auf historische Waffen (das alte Zeug).

Unsere Planungs- und Einbauzeit – 2018 bis 2020 – war nicht so langwierig wie bei der anderen Dauerausstellung. Fast alle Groß- und Kleingeräte wurden und werden hier seit Jahrzehnten als Leihgaben des Dresdner Militärhistorischen Museums ausgestellt. Die bisherige locker-traditionelle Präsentationsform war zwar bei den Besuchern sehr beliebt, aber sie hatte den großen Nachteil, daß die auf ihren hölzernen Lafetten oder auf Sandsteinblöcken liegenden Kanonenrohre problemlos berührt werden konnten. Dieser Umstand sollte bei der Neuplanung eingeschränkt werden. Auch war die Ausstellung nach mehr als 20 Jahren Standzeit materiell verschlissen, die Texte waren nur deutschsprachig, und mediale Informationsangebote gab es bisher in diesem Raum überhaupt nicht.

Die baulichen Renovierungsarbeiten beschränkten sich auf partielle Putzerneuerung, Malerarbeiten und Ertüchtigung der Elektroanlagen (einschließlich neuer Nachtspeicheröfen und Raumlampen) im Erdgeschoßraum. Teilsanierungen des Gesamtgebäudes hatten schon in den Jahren davor immer wieder stattgefunden.

Zur Geschichte des Gebäudes

»Altes Zeughaus: erbaut 1594 im Stil der Renaissance; diente der Aufbewahrung von Waffen und Kriegsgerät aller Art, außer Pulver; Saal im Erdgeschoß mit Kreuzgewölben und toskanischen Säulen geschmückt; im Obergeschoß nach 1871 Einbau von Gefangenenzellen zur Unterbringung von Zivilgefangenen.« (Angelika Taube.)

Kurfürst Christian I. von Sachsen hatte – wegen der Veränderungen in allen waffentechnischen Bereichen – den Ausbau des Königsteins zur Landesfestung in Auftrag gegeben. Der Entwurf des Alten Zeughauses stammt vom damaligen Oberzeug- und Festungsbaumeister Paul Buchner.

Für die Neugestaltung stand uns nur das Erdgeschoß des stattlichen, zweigeschossigen Gebäudes mit dreigeschossigem Dachstuhl zur Verfügung. Obwohl der Raum nicht sehr hoch ist, besitzt er mit seinen drei dicken, leicht bauchigen Mittelsäulen, die auf kräftig ausgebildeten Steinsockeln stehen und in wulstigen Kapitellen mit Deckplatten enden, von wo aus die eleganten Kreuzgrate der Gewölbedecke ausstrahlen, eine besonders intensive Aura. Auch sein Boden aus Sandsteinplatten trägt dazu bei.

Eine bauhistorische Besonderheit des Alten Zeughauses besteht übrigens in einem rechteckigen, seitlich angebauten und mit Sandsteinstufen ausgestatteten, einläufigen Treppenhaus. Um den Transport militärischer Geräte zu erleichtern, hatte Paul Buchner auf die bisher übliche Wendeltreppe verzichtet.

In unserem Entwurf wurden alle Großgeräte – Kanonenrohre mit und ohne Lafette, Mörser, Kugeln und Munitionswagen – in einem großen, zentralen, rechteckigen Raumbereich zusammengefaßt und mit einem umlaufenden, auf massiven Sandsteinsockeln ruhenden, niedrigen Geländerband aus Stahl umgeben. Auf der Oberseite des Bandes sind alle Objektbeschriftungen in drei Sprachen gut lesbar angebracht. (Graphik: Peter Mauksch.) Vor den Außenwänden stehen zwischen den Fenstern auf jeder Seite drei große, geöffnete Vitrinenschränke. Im indirekt beleuchteten, tiefen Hohlraum der Vitrinen sind kleinere militärische Geräte, eine Uniform und Modelle ausgestellt. Auf den geöffneten Schranktüren sind die neuen Erläuterungstexte und manchmal auch die Medien (Bildschirme) verteilt. Jeder Vitrinenschrank ist einem speziellen Thema der Gebäude- und Artillerie-Geschichte gewidmet. Verfaßt wurden die Texte von Ingo Busse, dem Kurator dieser Ausstellung. Die Oberleitung lag, wie immer, bei der Geschäftsführerin Angelika Taube.

Auch der Kassentresen mit moderner Technik mußte neu entworfen und gebaut werden, ebenso wie eine Pädagogikecke. Hier wird in einer waagrecht angebrachten Wand-Pultvitrine die Zusammensetzung des Schwarzpulvers erläutert. Unweit davon, auf einer niedrigen Ausstellungsfläche, steht ein Pulverfaß, an dem man riechen kann, daneben liegt eine Kanonenkugel (Bombe), deren Hohlraum einst mit Schwarzpulver gefüllt wurde. Um das Gewicht des Metalls zu spüren, wurde eine Kugel aufgeschnitten. Das Kugelsegment läßt sich anheben (und zurücklegen!). Für diese interaktiven Objekte und alle Kindertexte an den einzelnen Vitrinen war die Museumspädagogin, die eigentlich Mittelalterhistorikerin ist, Maria Pretzschner, zuständig.

Im gemauerten Erdgeschoß lagerten früher die Großgeräte, im Obergeschoß mit seinen Holzstützen und Dielenböden die leichten Feuer-, Hieb- und Stichwaffen, Munition, Lunten, Kugelblei, Werkzeuge und die Grundstoffe für die Pulverherstellung. Das Pulver wurde in separaten, gut gesicherten Pulvermagazinen aufbewahrt.

Die Verzierungen und Wappen an den aus Bronze gegossenen Kanonenrohren weisen mehr auf den Stolz der Auftraggeber und Besitzer hin als auf militärische Potenz, Zielgenauigkeit und Durchschlagskraft.

Mörser dienten zum Beschuß des Nahbereichs der Festung (auf Feinde, die sich den Festungsmauern bis auf 300 m angenähert hatten).

Nur selten kamen diese Waffen hier auf der Festung zum kriegerischen Einsatz. Hauptsächlich wurde zu Ehren hoher Gäste und bei Königsgeburtstagen aus Kanonenrohren (»blind«) geschossen.

1. Das Alte Zeughaus von Südosten.

1. The Old Armoury from the south-east.

Old Armoury, 2018–20

As an accompaniment to our long-term exhibition in the Gatehouse and in the close-range defence, which recounts the political, social, and architectonic history of the Fortress, here focus on historical weapons (the old stuff).

Our planning and installation time – 2018 to 2020 – did not drag on as much as the other long-term exhibition. Almost all of the large and small equipment had been exhibited here for decades as loans from the Dresden Bundeswehr Military History Museum . The previously loosely traditional presentation form was very popular with visitors, but it had the great disadvantage that all of the cannons, which were lying on their wooden gun carriages or on sandstone blocks, were open to being touched. The new plan aimed to restrict the possibilities for this. In addition, the exhibition, after being in place for more than 20 years, was materially worn. The texts were only in German, and there were no other information media at all in this space.

Architectural renovation was restricted to partial renewal of the plaster, painting work, and retrofitting of the electrical installations (including new night storage heaters and space lamps) in the ground storey space. Partial renovations of the whole building had repeatedly taken place over the previous years.

On the history of the building

»Old Armoury: built in 1594 in the Renaissance style; served as a store for weapons and war gear of all kinds, except for powder; a hall on the ground storey adorned with cross vaults and Tuscan pillars; prisoners' cells were installed in the upper storey after 1871 to house civilian prisoners.« (Angelika Taube.)

Following the changes in all areas of weaponry technology, Prince Elector Christian I of Saxony commissioned the expansion of the Königstein to create a regional fortress. The Old Armoury was designed by the master armoury and fortress builder of the time, Paul Buchner.

For the redesign, we had only the ground storey of this imposing two-storey building with its three-storey roof truss. Although the space is not very high, it possesses an especially intense aura, with its three thick, slightly bulbous central pillars, which stand on massively constructed stone pedestals and end in bulging capitals with ceiling plates from which the elegant cross ridges of the vaulted ceiling radiate. This aura is also contributed to by the sandstone flooring slabs.

One peculiarity of the Old Armory in architectural history terms, incidentally, is the rectangular stairwell, which is built on to the side and is equipped with sandstone steps. Paul Buchner dispensed with the usual spiral staircase in order to make transporting the military equipment easier.

In our design, all of the large equipment – cannons with and without gun carriages, mortars, cannon balls and munition wagons – are gathered together in a large, central, rectangular area, surrounded by a continuous low railing band of steel resting on massive sandstone pedestals. Affixed to the upper side of the band are the signs labelling every object, in three languages and easily legible. (Graphic: Peter Mauksch.) On every side, in front of the outer walls and between the windows, are three large, open glass cabinet cases. In the indirectly-illuminated, deep hollow space of the glass cases, smaller items of military equipment, a uniform, and models are displayed. The new explanatory texts – and, in some cases, the media screens – are distributed around the open cabinet doors. Each glass cabinet is dedicated to a specific theme within the histories of architecture and artillery. The texts were composed by Ingo Busse, curator of this exhibition. As always, overall leadership rested with managing director Angelika Taube.

The cash desk with modern technology had to be specially designed and built, along with the educational corner. In a horizontally-arranged wall console glass case, the composition of gunpowder is explained. Not far away from it, on a low exhibition surface, is a powder keg where one can smell the powder. Next to it is a cannon ball (a bombshell); once, the hollow space within it would have been filled with powder. A ball has been cut into in order to get a sense of the weight of the metal; this section of a ball can be lifted (and laid back down!). The museum educator Maria Pretzschner – who is actually a mediaeval historian – was responsible for these interactive objects and for all the texts for children in the individual glass cases.

The brickwork ground storey was formerly used to store the large equipment, whereas the upper storey, with its wooden supports and board floors, was used for the light firearms, bladed sidearms, munitions, slow matches, bullet lead, tools, and the materials for making gunpowder. The powder was stored in separate well-secured powder magazines.

The decorations and coats of arms on the bronze-cast cannon barrels speak more for the pride of those who commissioned and owned them than for their military potency, accuracy of aim, or force.

Mortars were used to bombard the area close to the Fortress (against enemies who had approached within 300 m of the Fortress walls).

These weapons here at the Fortress were rarely used in military action. They were used mainly to honour distinguished guests and mark the birthdays of royalty by firing off cannons (»blanks«).

Bilder 1–4
Nachfolgend einige Zitate aus den Erläuterungstexten an den »Schrankwänden« (von Ingo Busse):

Artillerie – Geschichte

Der Begriff Artillerie geht auf das altfranzösische ›*artillier*‹ zurück und bedeutet: mit Kriegsgerät bestücken. Er umfaßt alle schweren Feuerwaffen und den Truppenteil, der sie bedient, doch auch die großen Kriegsmaschinen der Antike und des frühen Mittelalters …

Artillerie – für Festungen

Die Festungsartillerie bestand hauptsächlich aus schweren Geschützen mit überwiegend großen Kalibern. Die Kanonen, Haubitzen und Mörser lagerten auf speziellen Lafetten, das Ladezeug daneben auf Kreuzblöcken. Festungskanonen waren meist länger und schwerer als Feldkanonen. Sie standen gedeckt hinter der Brustwehr und feuerten durch Schießscharten …

Artillerie – Technik

Zu den Geschützen der historischen Artillerie zählten Kanonen (mit langem Rohr) zum Beschuß entfernt liegender Ziele, Mörser (Steilfeuerwaffen mit sehr kurzem Rohr) zum indirekten Beschuß und Haubitzen (mit Rohren mittlerer Länge) sowohl für den direkten als auch den indirekten Beschuß entfernt liegender Ziele. Sie alle gab es in verschiedenen Größen und Kalibern, d. h. mit unterschiedlichen Innendurchmessern des Rohres …

Die Nahverteidigung der Festung Königstein

In den Inventarlisten des Königsteins finden sich stets große Mengen an Handfeuerwaffen, Munition und Ausrüstungsgegenständen für das Fußvolk bzw. für die Infanterie sowie Tausende vorbereiteter Handgranaten …

Die Fernverteidigung der Festung Königstein

Die auf dem Tafelberg gelegene Festung war mit zahlreichen Geschützen ausgestattet. Sie standen einsatzbereit an der Ringmauer oder im Alten Zeughaus. Schon kurz nach ihrer Entstehung, 1598, verfügte die Festung Königstein über 28 Kanonen und drei Mörser. 1633, während des Dreißigjährigen Krieges, waren es 83 Kanonen und neun Mörser, 1756, zu Beginn des Siebenjährigen Krieges, 93 Kanonen, 42 Mörser und eine Haubitze …

Pictures 1–4
Following: a number of quotations from the explanatory texts on the »cupboard walls« (by Ingo Busse):

Artillery – a history

The term artillery is derived from the old French word ›*artillier*‹, and means »to stock with military equipment«. It describes all heavy firearms and the personnel within an army that operate them, but also the great war machines of antiquity and of the early mediaeval age …

Artillery – for fortresses
The fortress artillery consisted primarily of heavy guns, primarily large-calibre. The cannons, howitzers, and mortars rest on special gun carriages, with the loading equipment beside them on cross blocks. Fortress cannons were generally longer and heavier than field cannons. They would stand concealed behind the parapet and fire through the embrasures …

Artillery – technology

The guns of historical artillery included cannons (with a long barrel) for firing upon targets at a distance, mortars (highangle firearms with a very short barrel) for indirect fire and howitzers (with barrels of medium length), used for direct bombardment, but also for indirect bombardment of distant targets. All of these existed in various sizes and calibres – that is, with different interior barrel dimensions …

The close-range defence of the Königstein Fortress

The inventories for the Königstein consistently show large volumes of handheld firearms, munitions, and other items of equipment for foot soldiers (infantry) and thousands of prepared hand grenades …

The remote-range defence of the Königstein Fortress

The Fortress located on the flat-topped mountain was equipped with numerous guns. They were positioned on the ring wall ready for use, or in the Old Armoury. Even shortly after its creation, in 1598, the Königstein Fortress already had 28 cannons and three mortars. In 1633, during the Thirty Years' War, there were 83 cannons and nine mortars, and in 1756, at the beginning of the Seven Years' War, there were 93 cannons, 42 mortars, and a howitzer …

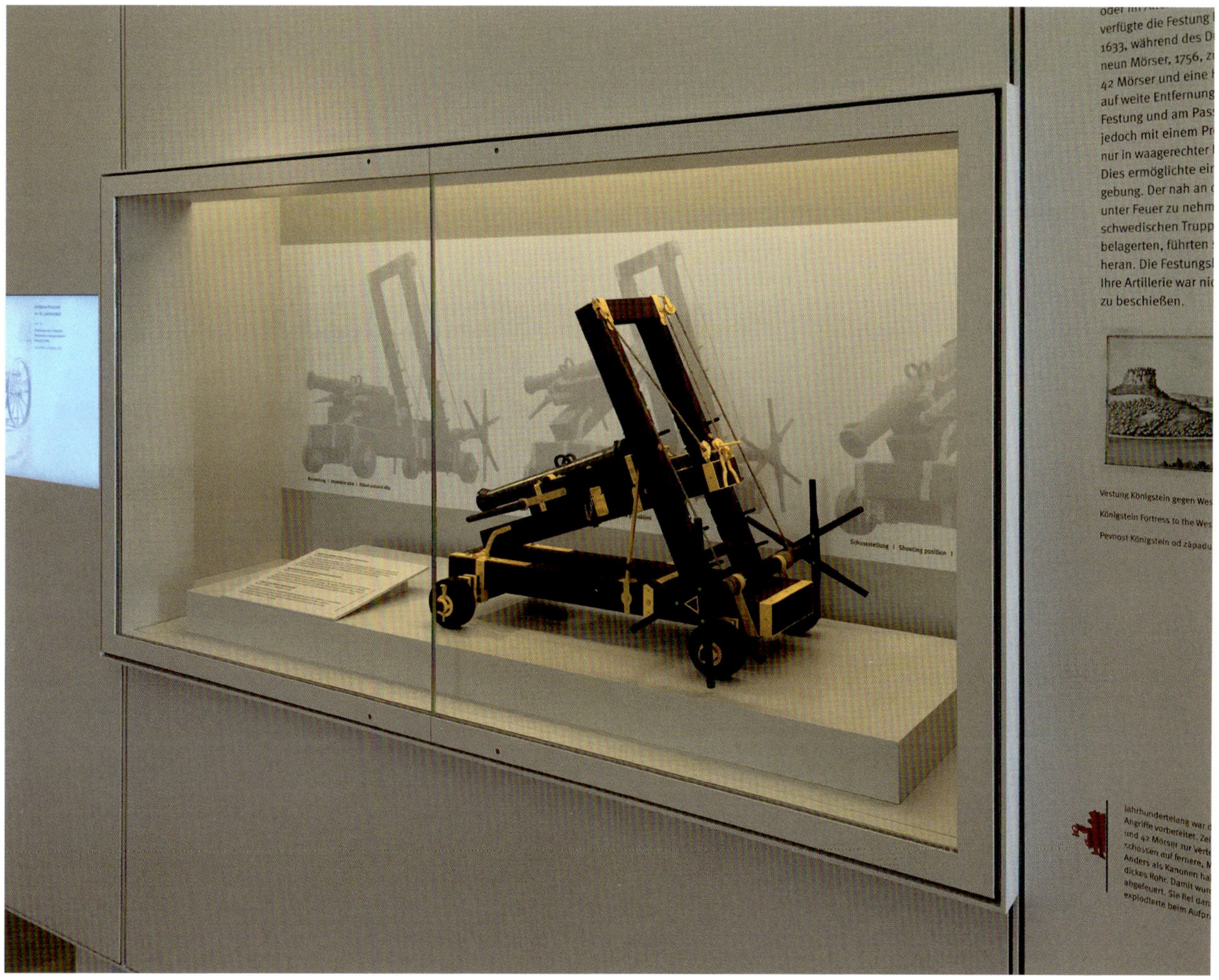

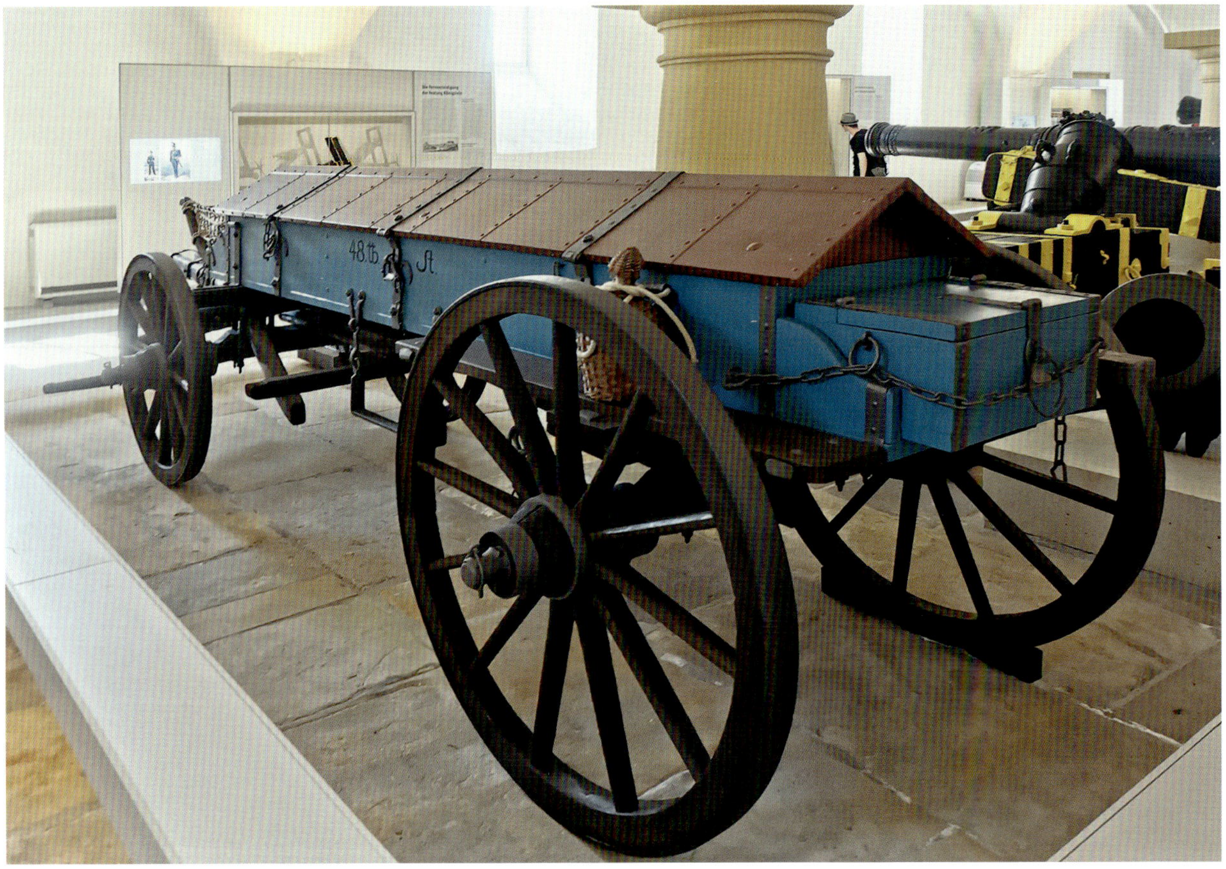

Bilder 5–7
Der von uns gestaltete Ausstellungsraum im Alten Zeughaus war übrigens bereits seit Beginn des 19. Jahrhunderts ein repräsentativer Schauraum. Touristische Besucher, die eine Genehmigung aus Dresden vorlegen konnten, durften – aber nur mit einem von der Festung zur Verfügung gestellten Führer – das Königsteinplateau betreten und einzelne Gebäude auch von innen besichtigen. Viele der hier ausgestellten Kanonen, Mörser, Kugeln und Gewehre waren militärisch damals bereits veraltet und hatten ausschließlich musealen Charakter.

Pictures 5–7
Incidentally, the exhibition space that we designed in the Old Armoury had been a grand display room since the early 19th century. Visiting tourists who could show a permit from Dresden were allowed to set foot on the Königstein plateau and to see inside individual buildings – but only if accompanied by one of the guides provided by the Fortress. Many of the cannons, mortars, balls, and guns exhibited here were already outdated in military terms, and were purely museum pieces.

1. Das Neue Zeughaus und das Kommandantenhaus von Südosten.
2. Entwurfsskizze für die Neugestaltung des Zugangs zum Neuen Zeughaus.
3. Neues Zeughaus, Grundriß und Schnitte.

1. The New Armoury and the commandant's house from the south-east.
2. Design sketch for the redesign of the entrance to the New Armoury.
3. New Armoury, floor plan and sections.

Neues Zeughaus, 2014–20
Dauerausstellung des Militärhistorischen Museums der Bundeswehr (MHM) unter dem Titel »Faszination Festung – Eine Geschichte des sicheren Ortes«

»Neues Zeughaus: 1631 als Johannissaal (Heldensaal) mit Längsachse über dem dunklen Aufgang errichtet; Festsaal, der gleichzeitig Verteidigungszwecken diente; deshalb Fußboden ehemals mit Falltüren versehen gewesen; nach Brand 1816 Wiederaufbau als Neues Zeughaus.« (Angelika Taube.)

Auf dem Photo oben ist der Außenzustand des Gebäudes nach Abschluß der Sanierungsarbeiten zu sehen. Die beiden mächtigen Kastanienbäume, die den Haupteingang zur alten Ausstellung des MHM markierten, wurden leider Opfer einer Baumkrankheit und mußten gefällt werden.

Das heutige Neue Zeughaus hatte – wie bereits erwähnt – einen Vorgängerbau, der nicht ganz so hoch war wie das jetzige Gebäude. Er wurde als Johannissaal nach den Plänen des Generalzeugmeisters und Obersten Johann Melchior von Schwalbach ab dem Jahr 1631 über der »Dunklen Appareille« erbaut. Dieser 40 m lange und 14 m breite Saal mit Dielenboden und Holzdecke war von den königlichen Wohnräumen im Torhaus ebenerdig zugänglich und diente vor allem repräsentativen Festen. Sie fanden hier mit Musik (Dresdner Hofkapelle), reichlich gedeckter Speisetafel, viel Wein und barocker Pracht (Kostüme!) im 17. und 18. Jahrhundert statt. Zur Unterhaltung wurden die Gäste gewogen: August der Starke wog im Jahr 1732, wenige Monate vor seinem Tod, 103 kg, der preußische Soldatenkönig Friedrich Wilhelm im Jahr 1728, damals war er 40 Jahre alt, 107 kg. An den Wänden hingen 112 Gemälde von »Generalspersonen«. Deswegen trug der größte Raum auf der Festung in der damaligen Zeit auch den Namen Heldensaal.

1806 wurde das Gebäude durch einen Dachstuhlbrand teilweise zerstört. 1816, nachdem Napoleons Armeen im Jahr zuvor in Waterloo endgültig besiegt worden waren, begann der Wiederaufbau als Neues Zeughaus.

In diesem Zusammenhang brach man die Freitreppe zum Haupteingang an der Ostseite ab und ersetzte sie durch eine Rampe. Statt der beiden schmalen, historischen Eingangstüren erhielt das Gebäude ein großes Tor, damit genügend Platz für die Einbringung von Kriegsgerät vorhanden war.

In den Grundmaßen entspricht der Neubau dem alten Bau. Nur die Decke wurde angehoben. Die Fenster ließ man unverändert. Sie sehen heute noch genauso aus wie zu Canalettos Zeiten.

Die neue, weiße Kreuzgrat-Gewölbedecke ruht im Innenraum auf zwei Stützenreihen mit insgesamt zwölf schmucklosen Pfeilern (ohne Sockelsteine und Kapitelle), so daß eine Art dreischiffige Hallenkirche entstand. Sie war jedoch weder als Kirche noch als Festsaal gedacht, sondern als Lagerhalle für militärische Großgeräte.

Die gesamte Festung entwickelte sich im Laufe des 19. Jahrhunderts mehr und mehr zu einer touristischen Attraktion – allerdings ohne ihren Festungscharakter im militärischen Sinne aufzugeben.

Nach 1871 wurde der Königstein als einzige sächsische Festung in das Festungssystem des Deutschen Reiches übernommen und zum Sperrfort ausgebaut.

New Armoury, 2014–20
Long-term exhibition of the Bundeswehr Military History Museum (MHM) entitled »The Fascination of the Fortress – A History of the Secure Place«

»New Armoury: built in 1631 as the Johannis Hall (Heroes Hall), with the longitudinal axis erected over the dark ascent; the banqueting hall, which also serves as a site for defence; for this reason, the floor was formerly equipped with trapdoors; rebuilt after a fire in 1816 as the New Armoury.« (Angelika Taube.)

The photo on the left shows the exterior condition of the building after completion of the renovation work. The two mighty chestnut trees that marked the main entrance to the old MHM exhibition unfortunately fell victim to tree disease and had to be cut down.

As has already been mentioned, today's New Armoury had a predecessor – a building that was not quite as high as the structure of today. It was built (as the Johannis Hall) based on plans by the general armoury master and Colonel Johann Melchior von Schwalbach starting in the year 1631 above the »Dunkle Appareille«. This 40 m long and 14 m wide hall with board floors and a wood ceiling was accessible at ground level from the royal apartments in the Gatehouse and was primarily used for grand feasts. In the 17th and 18th centuries, these were celebrated with music (by the Dresden court orchestra), amply decked tables, lots of wine, and baroque splendour (especially the clothing!). For amusement, the guests were weighed: in 1732, a few months before his death, August the Strong weighed 103 kg, in 1728, at the age of forty, the Prussian Soldier King Friedrich Wilhelm weighed 107 kg. On the walls hung 112 paintings of »general persons«. This is why the largest room in the Fortress was also known at the time as the Heroes Hall.

In 1806, the building was partially destroyed by a fire in the roof timbers. In 1816, a year after Napoleon's armies were finally defeated at Waterloo, work began on the rebuilding of what was to become the New Armoury.

It was in this context that the open-air staircase leading to the main entrance on the east side was demolished and replaced with a ramp. Instead of the two narrow historic entrance doors, the building received a large gate, ensuring ample clearance for bringing military equipment in.

The basic dimensions of the new building correspond to those of the old building. Only the ceiling was raised. The windows were left unchanged. They appear today just as they did in Canaletto's time.

In the interior space, the new white cross-ridge vault ceiling rests on two rows of supports with a total of twelve unadorned pillars (with no pedestals or capitals), creating a kind of three-naved hall church. This building, however, was intended neither as a church nor as a banqueting hall, but as a storage hall for large-scale military equipment.

Over the course of the 19th century the whole Fortress increasingly became a tourist attraction – although it did not lose its character as a military fortress.

After 1871, the Königstein was incorporated into the fortress system of the German Reich – as the only fortress in Saxony – and was developed into a stronghold.

Entsprechend der Pfeileranzahl und damit der Fenster, Fensternischen (im Innenraum von Rundbögen überwölbt) und der gemauerten Fensterzwischenräume wurden zwölf Themenkomplexe in den Raum eingegliedert:
1. Aggression und (Selbst-)Schutz.
2. Die Burg als Schutzbau, Symbol- und Sehnsuchtsort.
3. Burgen, Bürger, Barrikaden.
4. Festungswerke und Festungskrieg der frühen Neuzeit.
5. Die Ausweitung der Kampfzone und die Nationalisierung des Krieges.
6. Asymmetrische Kriege.
7. Materialschlachten und Grabenkrieg im Ersten Weltkrieg.
8. Luftkrieg und fliegende Festungen.
9. Atomarer Overkill.
10. Die Festung als Gefängnis, als Konzentrations- und Vernichtungslager.
11. Die Stadt als Festung im Zweiten Weltkrieg.
12. Sicherheitskonzepte des 21. Jahrhunderts, High-Tech-Krieger und Blauhelmsoldaten.

Twelve theme complexes were set up within the room; this corresponds to the number of pillars and thus the windows, the window niches (beneath the vaults of the round arches) and the masonry sections between the windows:
1. Aggression and (self)protection.
2. The castle as a protective structure, a symbolic place, and a yearned-for place.
3. Castles, citizens, barricades.
4. Fortification works and fortress war of the early modern period.
5. The expansion of the war zone and the nationalising of war.
6. Asymmetrical wars.
7. Material battles and trench warfare in the First World War.
8. Aerial war and flying fortresses.
9. Atomic overkill.
10. The fortress as prison, as concentration and extermination camp.
11. The city as a fortress in the Second World War.
12. Security concepts of the 21st century: high-tech warriors and blue helmet soldiers.

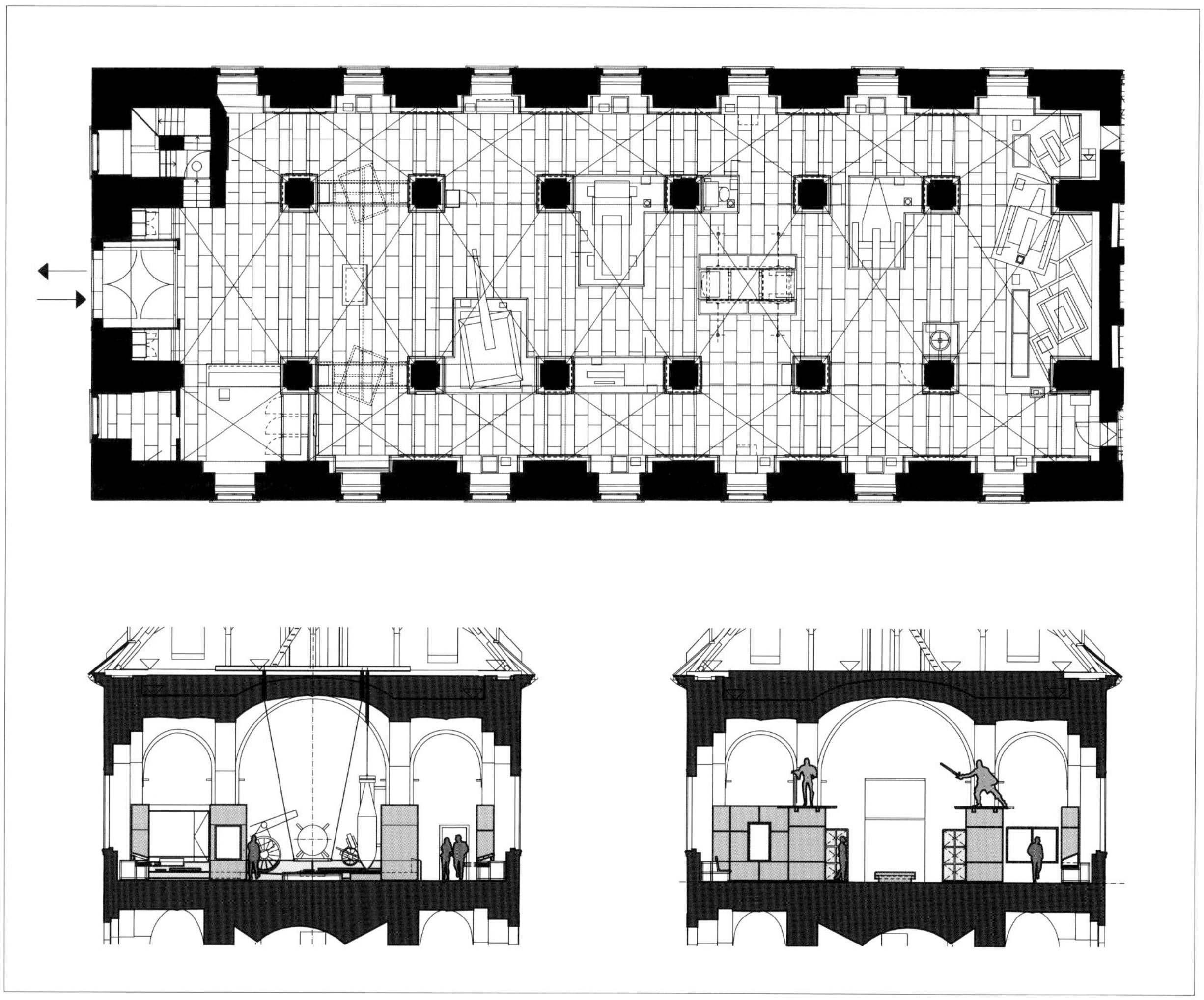

Bild 3
Als Eingangsbild schlug ich die Gegenüberstellung zweier Kämpfer aus unterschiedlichsten Zeiten vor: einen mittelalterlichen Ritter mit erhobenem, kampfbereitem Schwert in der rechten, metallgeschützten Hand (neu hergestellt von dem Plattner René Kohlstruck der Hamburger Firma Freyhand) und – gegenüber – einen supermodernen, vielleicht künstlich ferngesteuerten Roboter-Kämpfer (High-Tech-Krieger, den das MHM von einem Hersteller in den USA angekauft hat). Die äußerliche Ähnlichkeit der beiden Krieger ist offensichtlich, trotzdem ist der Roboter-Soldat, wie jeder weiß, seinem Kollegen aus dem Mittelalter kriegstechnisch weit überlegen. Bevor er in den Nahkampf eintreten würde, hätte er seinen Gegner mit Schüssen aus Maschinengewehren längst erledigt oder mit Laserstrahlen zum Schmelzen gebracht.

Unter diesem, auf Plattformen in 3 m Höhe plazierten, ungleichen Kriegerpaar ließ ich auf dem Boden aus Sandsteinplatten der Halle eine leicht geneigte Texttafel anbringen, auf die ein Zitat von Anne Frank gedruckt wurde. (Graphik: Anett Breite, überarbeitet vom MHM durch Katrin Miklich.) Es lautet: »Im Menschen ist nun mal ein Drang zum Totschlagen, zum Morden und Wüten, und so lange die ganze Menschheit, ohne Ausnahme, keine Metamorphose durchläuft, wird der Krieg wüten, wird alles, was gebaut, gepflegt und gewachsen ist, wieder abgeschnitten und vernichtet, und dann fängt es wieder von vorne an.«

Bild 1
Blick in den Saal des Neuen Zeughauses, wie er von 1989 an zu besichtigen war. Vor allem in den Seitenschiffen herrschte, mit kreuz und quer stehenden Großgeräten und Wandteilen, ein leicht verspieltes Chaos.

Bild 2
Die großen, hinterleuchteten Text- und Abbildungstafeln zu den zwölf Themenstationen wurden – wie auch das gesamte Ausstellungskonzept – von einem Team um den Hauptkurator und Ideengeber Gorch Pieken, der damals noch wissenschaftlicher Direktor des Dresdner MHM war, geschrieben und zusammengestellt. Die Gruppe sammelte auch passende Ausstellungsobjekte für die Vitrinen aus dem Besitz des MHM.

Im Ausstellungsentwurf wurden formal zwei wichtige Aspekte verarbeitet: zum einen (in den Seitenschiffen) die klar gegliederte Ordnung, wie sie innerhalb militärischer Strukturen herrscht. Eine »uniformierte Wand« mit Text-Photo-Tafel reiht sich an die andere, ähnlich einer Soldatenformation, die sich zum Appell aufgestellt hat. Ebenso verhält es sich mit den Pultvitrinen, die in die vorgebauten Fensterbrüstungen eingelassen sind.

Im Mittelschiff gibt es – wie in alten Kirchen und Museen üblich – keine ordnende Durchblicksachse. Alle historischen und modernen Großgeräte wurden gegeneinander versetzt und damit unregelmäßig aufgestellt – und zwar so, daß jeder Besucher den Eindruck von gestörter Symmetrie und damit von (stummer) Dissonanz erhält.

Picture 1
A view of the hall of the New Armoury, as it could be viewed from 1989 onwards. In the side naves in particular, a somewhat playful chaos predominates, with sections of wall and items of large equipment arranged in a criss-cross way.

Picture 2
The large backlit textual and illustrated panels for the twelve theme stations – and, indeed, the whole exhibition concept – are composed by a team headed by the chief curator and idea originator Gorch Pieken, who was still scientific director of the Dresden MHM at the time. The group also collected suitable exhibition objects for the glass cases from the MHM's reserves.

In terms of form, the exhibition design addresses two significant aspects. On the one hand, there is a clearly delineated order of the kind found within military structures (seen in the side naves). One »uniformed wall« with panels showing text and photos follows another, resembling a formation of soldiers on parade. The situation is similar with the desk-type glass cases set into the projecting window parapets.

In the central nave, there is no continuous axis of vision to impose order (as is usual for old churches and museums). All of the historical and modern large equipment items are irregularly arranged, at odd angles to each other – giving all visitors the impression of disrupted symmetry and thus of (silent) dissonance.

Picture 3
For an opening image, I proposed a coming-together of two warriors from different eras: a mediaeval knight with a sword raised ready for battle in his right hand, which is gloved in metal (newly created by the plate armourer René Kohlstruck from the Hamburg firm of Freyhand) and – opposite him – a supermodern, possibly remote-controlled robot soldier (a high-tech warrior purchased by the MHM from a manufacturer in the USA). The external resemblance between the two warriors is very apparent; in spite of this, the robot soldier is, as everyone knows, far superior to his colleague from the Middle Ages in terms of war technology. Before engaging in a hand-to-hand-combat, he would have finished his opponent with machine gun fire, or melted him with laser beams.

Beneath this unequal pair of warriors placed on platforms at a 3-m elevation, I had a slightly inclined text panel installed in the sandstone panel floor. It is printed with a quotation from Anne Frank. (Graphic: Anett Breite, reworked for MHM by Katrin Miklich.) It reads: » In human beings, there is a compulsion to strike down, to murder and rage, and as long as the whole of humanity, without exception, has not undergone a metamorphosis, war will rage, cutting down and annihilating that which has been built, tended, and grown, only for it to start all over again.«

Bild 4
Wie eine große beunruhigende, aber gleichzeitig auch beruhigende Bedrohung hat sich in der Mittelachse des Saales die Hülle einer Atombombe breitgemacht. An dünnen Stahlseilen hängt sie von der Decke herab. Ihre genaue Bezeichnung lautet ganz nüchtern: »Thermonuklearbombe Mk53, 2500 kg«.

Bild 5
Rechts im Vordergrund ein originalgroßes Holzmodell der neuesten Waffenentwicklung. Diese Kanone mit der Bezeichnung »Mantis« wurde zur Flugabwehr entwickelt und sollte die festungsartigen Feldlager der deutschen Bundeswehr in Afghanistan sichern.

Bild 6
Am Kopfende des ehemaligen Johannissaals und jetzigen Neuen Zeughauses wurde, vor dem gemalten Wanddenkmal der Festungskommandanten, eine breite Schräge errichtet, auf der ältere Feuerwaffen ausgestellt sind.

Picture 4
Like a vast and unsettling – and at the same time comforting – threat the shell of a nuclear bomb has come to rest in the central axis of the hall. It hangs down from the ceiling on thin steel cables. Its precise designation is, prosaically, »thermo-nuclear bomb Mk53, 2500 kg«.

Picture 5
On the right in the foreground is an original-size wooden model of the most recent development in weapons. Designated »Mantis«, this gun was developed for air defence, intended to protect the fortress-like military camps of the German Bundeswehr in Afghanistan.

Picture 6
At the head end of the former Johannis Hall, today the New Armoury, in front of the painted wall memorial to the fortress commanders, a wide slope was set up, on which older firearms are displayed.

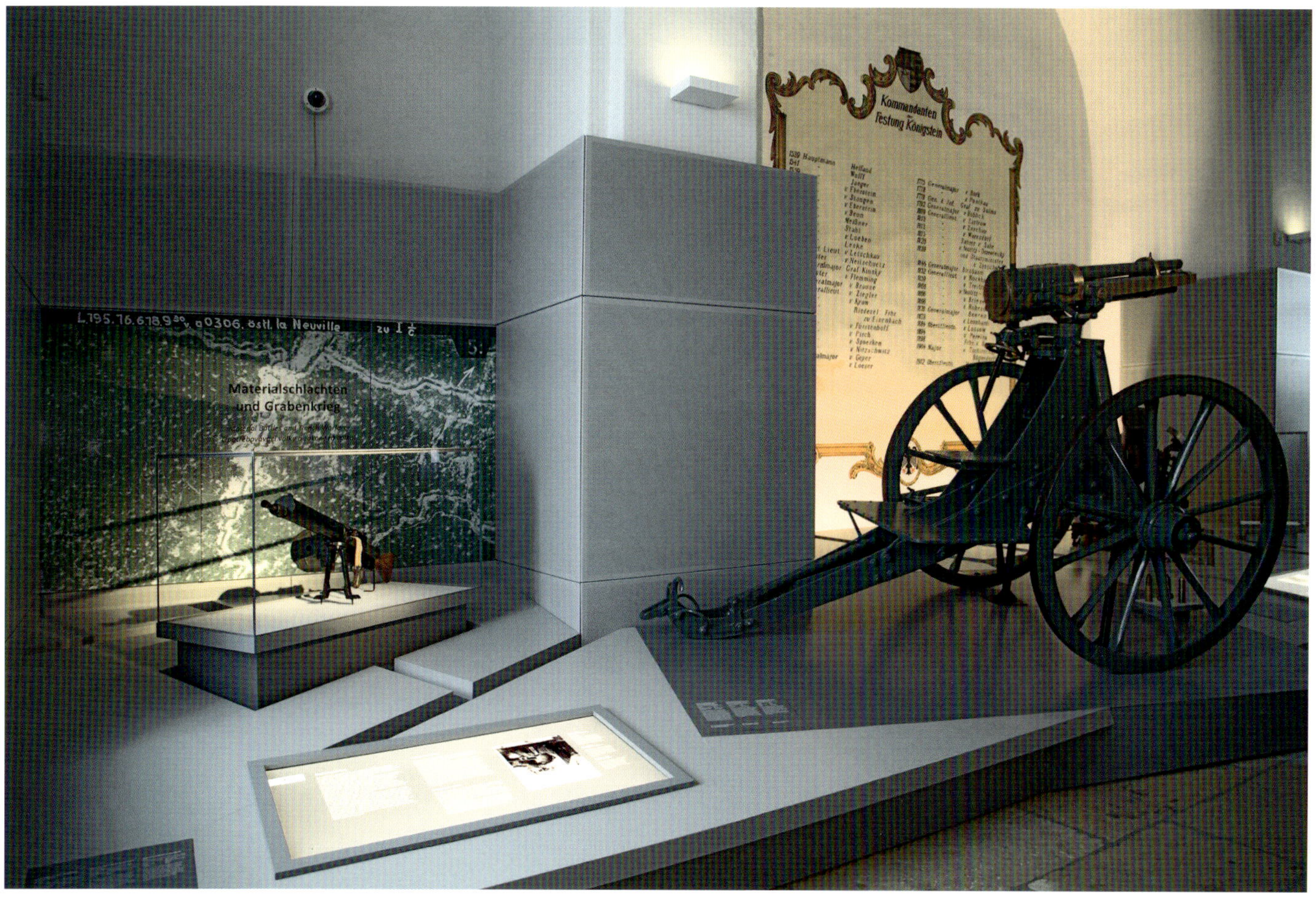

Brunnenhaus, 2015–18

Auch das Brunnenhaus hat eine lange Geschichte und einige Vorgängerbauten. Es begann mit der bereits erwähnten Abteufung des Brunnenschachts in den massiven Sandsteinfelsen des Königsteins unter der Leitung von Martin Planer im Jahr 1563. Niemand wußte zu diesem Zeitpunkt, wie tief das Loch, mit seinem Durchmesser von 3,5 m, letztlich gemeißelt werden mußte. Erst nach über fünf Jahren stießen die Bergleute in einer Tiefe von 139 m auf eine stärker wasserführende Schicht. 1569 beendete Planer bei einer Brunnentiefe von 152,5 m die Arbeit und übergab das Werk seinem Bauherrn, Kurfürst August von Sachsen. Heute gehört der Königstein-Brunnen mit dem Kyffhäuser-Brunnen (176 m) zu den tiefsten historischen Brunnen Europas.

Zunächst wurde ein hölzernes Hebewerk, genannt »Göpel«, mit einer kreisrunden Laufbahn für ein bis zwei Pferde zur Wasserförderung eingerichtet. Bereits nach wenigen Jahren war die Anlage, wegen unsachgemäßen Gebrauchs, marode. Der Dresdner Zeugmeister Paul Buchner schlug statt dessen ein Tretrad mit einem Durchmesser von 7 m vor.

Die Hebetechnik war nach dem Einbau des Tretrads zwar effektiver, aber für die Menschen, die auf der Festung dafür eingesetzt wurden, sehr mühsam.

»Vier Männer mußten darin täglich 28 800 Schritte laufen, um 36 Fässer mit jeweils 150 Litern Wasser zu fördern.« (Kurator der Ausstellung: Ingo Busse.)

Seit 1716 schützte ein Gebäude des Oberlandbaumeisters Pöppelmann den Festungsbrunnen.

Da diesem Brunnenhaus aus finanziellen Gründen das bombenfeste Gewölbe fehlte, beauftragte Kurfürst Friedrich August II. 1735 seinen seit 1728 in Dresden als Generalintendant der Zivil- und Militärgebäude am Hof verantwortlichen Architekten Jean de Bodt mit dem Entwurf eines absolut sicheren Brunnenhauses. Dieser Bau steht – immer wieder ergänzt und renoviert – bis heute.

Von außen erhielt das Gebäude – wie zur Tarnung – ein profanes, stattlich-bürgerliches Aussehen im klassizistisch angehauchten Barockstil. Unter dem an der östlichen Längsseite auf Wandlisenen ruhenden, über die Dachschräge hinausragenden, flachen Giebel mit Wappenrelief ist nur bei genauem Hinschauen zu erkennen, daß die mittlere Fensterreihe im oberen Fassadenbereich aus gemalten Attrappen besteht. Dahinter errichtete Jean de Bodt im Innern eine 4 m starke Gewölbedecke aus Sandsteinblöcken mit einer Spannweite von 10 m über der Brunnenanlage mit ihrem Tretrad. »Am 5. April 1871 hielt die damals moderne Technik auch im Brunnenhaus Einzug. Der Maschinenfabrikant Petzoldt aus Döhlen übergab der Garnisonverwaltung eine zum Wasserziehen bestimmte Dampfmaschine. Diese löste das bis dahin in Betrieb gewesene Tretrad ab.« (Angelika Taube.)

Und weiter: »Bei all den rein militärischen Neubauten vergaß man auch nicht die Sicherung des Brunnens. Immerhin war dieser weiterhin das ›Herz‹ der Festung. Deshalb wurde 1889 unter Beibehaltung des Sandsteingewölbes unmittelbar über dem Brunnen eine auf Eisenträgern ruhende Granitstampfbetondecke eingezogen.« (Angelika Taube.)

1892 erhielt das Brunnenhaus eine elektrische Beleuchtungsanlage und 1912 einen Elektromotor für die Wasserförderung. Im Jahr 1967 wurde der Brunnen stillgelegt und die Festung an die allgemeine Trinkwasserversorgung angeschlossen.

Für mich ist dieser Einbau mehr als eine Rekonstruktion. Ich sehe darin eher eine Kunstinstallation. Das Interessante an dem Rad ist – neben der Tatsache des In-die-Wand-gedrückt-Seins – sein Verhältnis zum Gesamtraum. Einerseits antwortet das Holzrad, formal perfekt angepaßt und ins Dreidimensionale erweitert, der steinernen Tonnenform des Deckengewölbes, andererseits scheint es durch seine enorme Größe die Enge des Raumes sprengen zu wollen. Dadurch entsteht beides: Harmonie und Dissonanz, erstarrte Ruhe, die jederzeit (fiktiv, in Gedanken) auch dynamisiert werden und den Raum zum Rotieren anregen könnte.

Mit der Achsen- und Rad-Rekonstruktion tritt noch ein weiterer Aspekt hinzu: nämlich der, daß der Raum und das umschlossene Raumvolumen die Tendenz zu einer Tunnel-Röhre erhalten. Man fühlt sich assoziativ – neben dem Gedanken an ein stark vergrößertes Hamsterrad – an eine Wassermühle erinnert, ein Riesenrad, eine Windturbine, einen Riesenventilator, eine moderne Tunnelbohrung oder ein zeppelinartiges Raumschiff, das in Wirklichkeit niemals aus Steinen gemauert oder aus Holz gebaut sein könnte. Hier, im Brunnenhaus auf der Festung, fehlen nur noch die passenden, raumgreifenden Musikklänge aus verschiedenen historischen Zeiten, aus Mittelalter, Renaissance, Barock, Gegenwart und Science-fiction-Weltallräumen, gemischt mit Geräuschen von sprudelndem Wasser oder fallenden Wassertropfen.

Aus romantischem Blickwinkel gesehen, haben wir es hier mit dem Gegenbild zum alten heimatverliebten Lied »Am Brunnen vor dem Tore« zu tun. Dieser Brunnen, mit seinem tiefen Loch, wurde – wie ein wertvoller Märchenschatz (mit sehr realistischer Funktionsbedeutung) – eingemauert, gesichert, getarnt und versteckt. Er liegt nicht mehr im Freien. Er bildet eine Festung in der Festung.

Kein Wunder, daß der glasgesicherte Brunnenschacht auch heute noch – einschließlich der Radinstallation – zu den touristischen Hauptsehenswürdigkeiten auf der Festung gehört.

1. Das Brunnenhaus von Nordosten.
2. Brunnen mit Wasserhebewerk (Tretrad). Kupferstich von Christoph Beichling, um 1840.
3. Blick in die Brunnentiefe beim Auffahren eines mit Wasser gefüllten Fasses (heute).

1. The Well House from the north-east.
2. Well with water hoist (treadwheel). Copper-plate engraving by Christoph Beichling, ca. 1840.
3. View into the depth of the well while driving up a barrel filled with water (today).

Well House, 2015–18

The Well House also has a long history; a number of buildings stood here before it. It began, as has already been mentioned, with the sinking of the well shaft into the massive sandstone rocks of the Königstein under the leadership of Martin Planer in 1563. At this point, no one knew how deep the hole, which is 3.5 m in diameter, would ultimately have to be carved. It was not until more than five years later that the miners struck a broader aquifer layer, at a depth of 139 m. In 1569, Planer halted the work, with the well at a depth of 152.5 m, and handed the workings over to his principal, Prince Elector August of Saxony. Today, the Königstein well, along with the Kyffhäuser well (176 m), is among the deepest historical wells in Europe.

At first, a wooden lifting tool named »Göpel« was set up, with a circular track for one or two horses, to bring water up from the well. This structure became dilapidated after only a few years, owing to improper use. The Dresden armoury master Paul Buchner suggested that a treadwheel with a diameter of 7 m be used instead.

After the installation of the treadwheel, the lifting technology was more effective, but it meant a lot of extremely hard work for the people employed for the purpose at the Fortress.

»Four people would have to achieve 28,800 steps daily, in order to produce 36 barrels, each containing 150 l of water.« (Curator of the exhibition: Ingo Busse.)

A building created by head regional master architect Pöppelmann has protected the Fortress well since 1716.

For financial reasons, this Well House lacks a bombproof vault. In 1735, Prince Elector Friedrich August II therefore commissioned the architect Jean de Bodt, who had been made general intendant of court civilian and military architecture in Dresden in 1728, to design an absolutely secure well house. This building still stands today – after numerous additions and renovations.

The building was given an exterior in a secular, grand baroque style – with a touch of classicism as a kind of camouflage. Beneath the flat gable with the coat of arms in relief resting on wall pilasters on the long side to the east, which projects beyond the incline of the roof, a close look will reveal that the central row of windows in the upper area of the façade consists of painted false windows. Behind them, in the interior, Jean de Bodt erected a 4 m thick vaulted ceiling of sandstone blocks with a span of 10 m above the well structure and its treadwheel. »On the 5th of April 1871, what was at the time modern technology was moved into the Well House. The machine manufacturer Petzoldt from Döhlen handed over to the garrison authorities a steam-powered machine designed for drawing water. It provided a replacement for the treadwheel that had been in operation here.« (Angelika Taube.)

Further more: »With all the purely military new architecture, the security of this well was not forgotten. After all, it was still the ›heart‹ of the Fortress. In 1889, whilst the sandstone vault was retained, a granite compressed concrete ceiling resting on iron supports was installed directly above the well.« (Angelika Taube.)

In 1892, the Well House was given an electrical lighting system, and an electrical motor for drawing water was installed in 1912. In 1967, operation of the well ceased, as the Fortress was connected to the public water supply.

For me, this installation is more than a reconstruction. I see it as more of an art installation. The interesting thing about the wheel – apart from the fact that it is pressed into the wall – is its relationship to the space as a whole. On the one hand, the wooden wheel, whose form is perfectly adapted and expanded into three dimensions, is a response to the stone barrel form. On the other hand, its enormous size makes it look as though it is inclined to explode the narrow room. As a result, both harmony and dissonance are created: a sense of a frozen stillness that might (albeit only fictionally) become dynamic at any moment and move the room to rotate.

The reconstruction of the wheel and its axle brings one further aspect: it gives the room and the enclosing room volume the tendency to appear like a tunnel or tube. By association, one is reminded (aside from the resemblance to a much-enlarged hamster wheel) of a watermill, a big wheel, a wind turbine, a giant ventilator, a modern tunnel bore or a zeppelin-like spaceship, which, in reality, could never be made by laying stones or constructed from wood. Here, in the Well House of the Fortress, all that is missing are the appropriate sounds of music to fill the space: music from various historic periods – the Middle Ages, the Renaissance, the baroque period, the present day, and outer space worlds of science fiction, mingling with the sounds of splashing water and falling drops of water.

Seen from a romantic perspective, we are faced here with the antithesis to the old song of love for home »Am Brunnen vor dem Tore« (»at the well before the gates«). This well, with its deep shaft, is walled up, secured, camouflaged, and concealed – like some priceless treasure in a fairy tale (but with a very real functional significance). It is no longer out in the open air. It constitutes a fortress within the Fortress.

It is no wonder that the glass-secured well shaft – including the wheel installation – is still one of the top tourist attractions at the Fortress today.

C. Beichling sc.

Bild 1

Unsere Installation erinnert an das ehemalige Tretrad mit seinem originalen Durchmesser. Da der Platz für den Einbau an der historisch richtigen Stelle im Raum – wegen der zu berücksichtigenden Besucher – nicht mehr vorhanden war, wurde der moderne, runde Holzfachwerkbau zum Teil (fiktiv) in die innere Raumwand »hineingedrückt«. Deswegen ist das Tretrad nicht mehr beweglich. Nur im oberen Bereich ist das originale Breitenmaß des alten Rades noch zu erkennen.

Die frühere Drehachse (der dicke, runde Holzbalken) befindet sich in der historisch richtigen Position. Die einstigen Auflager – schon vor vielen Jahren abgeschlagen – rekonstruierten wir mit Stahlwinkeln (an den Originalstellen).

Im hinteren Bereich des sehr schmalen Raumes stellten wir eine kleine, hohe Vitrine auf, in der ein neues Modell des Brunnens (von Paul Wells) gezeigt wird. Man sieht hier den Vorgang des »Abteufens«, des Brunnenausmeißelns. Oben, über dem Brunnen, steht jene einfache Holzüberdachung, die den Brunnenschacht vor äußeren Einflüssen schützen sollte.

Auf einem Bildschirm in der Nähe des Eingangs ist eine heutige Kamerafahrt in die Tiefe des Brunnenschachts zu sehen. Auf einem zweiten Bildschirm rechts neben der Rekonstruktion des Tretrads wird in einer Animation die monotone Tätigkeit der einstigen Tretrad-Arbeiter gezeigt. Oft waren es Fronarbeiter, Soldaten oder Gefangene, die hier oben in kalten Arrestzellen ihre Strafe absaßen.

Bilder 2, 3

Entwurfsskizzen zur Rekonstruktion des Tretrads.

Bild 4

Wasserfördertechnik in ihrem heutigen Zustand. Im Sommerhalbjahr täglich bei Führungen aktiviert.

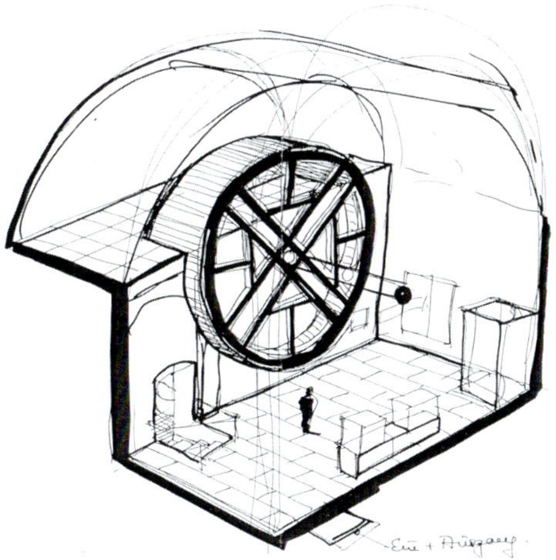

Picture 1
Our installation recalls the former treadwheel, and has the same diameter as the original wheel. Because there was no longer enough space for the installation at the historically correct site (as the needs of visitors had to be taken into account), the modern round wooden framework construction is partially »pressed« into the interior wall of the space (a fictional element). This means that the treadmill can no longer be moved. Only in the upper area are the original dimensions of the old wheel still recognisable.

The previous axis of rotation (the thick, round wooden beam) is located in the historically correct position. We reconstructed the previous cradle – dismantled several years ago – using steel angles (in the original places).

In the rear area of this very narrow room, we set up a small, high glass case, in which was displayed a new model of the well (by Paul Wells). Here, you can see the process of »sinking« or chiselling the well. Above, over the well, is the simple wooden roofing, intended to protect the well shaft from outside influences.

On a screen close to the entrance, modern-day footage from a camera travelling down the well shaft can be seen. A second screen on the right next to the reconstructed treadwheel shows, as an animation, the monotonous routine of those who once worked the treadwheel. They were often serfs, soldiers, or captives, serving their sentence in the cold cells here above.

Pictures 2, 3
Design sketches for reconstruction of the treadwheel.

Picture 4
The current state of water-drawing technology. In the summer half-year, it is activated daily for the tours.

Johann-Georgenburg, 2015–21

Dauerausstellung in den ehemaligen Küchenräumen der Johann-Georgenburg zum Thema »Gefangen auf dem Königstein«, dazu weitere Einbauten im Erdgeschoß des Hauptgebäudes der Burg

»Georgenburg: im Mittelalter als Kaiserburg (…) bezeichneter Teil der Burganlage (…); später umgebaut und 1619 als Georgenburg im Renaissancestil neu eingeweiht; anfangs als Jagdschlößchen, später als Staatsgefängnis genutzt.« (Angelika Taube.)

Für unsere Dauerausstellung zum Thema »Staatsgefängnis« konnten wir die vom Innenhof über wenige nach unten führende Stufen zugänglichen ehemaligen Küchenräume der alten Johann-Georgenburg nutzen. Die meisten Arrestzellen befanden sich in den Obergeschossen.

Johann Georg Castle, 2015–21

Long-term exhibition in the former kitchen spaces of the Johann Georg Castle on the theme »Imprisoned on the Königstein«, also further installations on the ground storey of the Johann Georg Castle main building

»Georg Castle: in the Middle Ages, it was an imperial castle (…) Designated part of the castle complex (…); later converted and rededicated in 1619 as the Georg Castle, in a new Renaissance style; initially as a small hunting lodge, later used as a state prison.« (Angelika Taube.)

For our long-term exhibition on the theme of the »state prison«, we used the former kitchen spaces of the old Johann Georg Castle, which are accessible from the inner courtyard via a small number of steps that lead downward. Most of the cells were located in the upper storeys.

1, 2. Die Johann-Georgenburg von Osten mit den später verglasten Arkaden.

1, 2. The Johann Georg Castle from the east with the later glazed arcades.

Bild 1
Im ersten Ausstellungsraum gehen die Besucher auf ein raumbreites Eisengitter zu. Hier, im hinteren Drittel des Raumes, unter dem breiten Gewölbebogen, soll durch das Bild des Gitters bei den Besuchern ein Gefühl oder besser eine Vorstellung von Gefangenschaft evoziert werden. Hinter dem Gitter liegt im Bodenbereich eine breite Vitrine »gefangen«, in der Bein- und Handeisen gezeigt werden. Manche der Gefangenen mußten sie Tag und Nacht tragen, auch während der Arbeit. Gefängnisinsassen der höheren Gesellschaftsschichten genossen gewisse Privilegien, die vom eigenen Diener bis zum individuellen Wunschessen reichten.

Über der Vitrine ist auf einem großen Bildschirm ein Film zu sehen, der die fiktive Einlieferung eines Gefangenen auf der Festung zeigt. (Drehbuch: Andrej Pawluschkow.) Mit der Ankunft erlosch für den Delinquenten (es waren größtenteils Männer) jede Art von Freiheit. Er mußte sich, zum Teil in Ketten gelegt, an die Anweisungen der bewaffneten Bewachungssoldaten halten. Das Verlassen der Arrestzellen war nur selten, unter strenger Aufsicht, erlaubt.

Bild 2
Durchgang zum nächsten Raum. Rechts neben der leicht spitzbogenförmigen Tür eine der Texttafeln, auf der in drei Sprachen die Geschichte des Staatsgefängnisses auf der Festung Königstein erläutert wird.

Picture 1
In the first exhibition room, visitors approach an iron grid that spans the full width of the room. Here, in the rearward third of the room, beneath the wide vault arch, the image of the grid is intended to evoke in visitors a feeling – or rather an impression – of being in prison. Behind the grid, at floor level, a wide glass case is »trapped«, in which hand and foot shackles are displayed. Some of those who were prisoners in the building had to wear these by day and by night, and also during their labours. Prison inmates from the higher social classes enjoyed certain privileges, ranging from their own servants to individual meals of their choice.

Above the glass case, on a big screen, a film is showing, portraying the fictional committal of a prisoner to the Fortress. (Script: Andrej Pawluschkow.) Upon arrival, the delinquents (largely men) lost every kind of freedom. They would have to obey the instructions of the guards, and would sometimes be in chains. They were permitted to leave their cells only rarely, and then only under close supervision.

Picture 2
Passage to the next room. On the right, next to the door with the slightly pointed arch shape, is one of the text panels, which explain the history of the state prison at the Königstein Fortress in three languages.

Bild 3
Seine Hoch-Zeit hatte das Staatsgefängnis im 18. und 19. Jahrhundert, als die meisten politischen Gefangenen hier einsaßen. Sie werden im zweiten Raum einzeln thematisiert. Auf der rechten schneeweißen Wand mit dem markanten Ansatz der überwölbenden Kreuzgratdecke wurde von uns eine hinterleuchtete Fläche mit 36 ausgewählten Porträtphotos von Gefangenen plaziert. (Kurator: Andrej Pawluschkow.) Manche von ihnen saßen nur wenige Wochen oder Monate auf der Festung in ihren Zellen, andere jahrelang, einige wenige sogar lebenslänglich.

Wie in Berlin, ja in ganz Europa, formierten sich auch in Dresden zwischen 1840 und 1850 aufgeklärte Bürger aus allen Schichten zu einer Demokratiebewegung. Sie wollten den Absolutheitsanspruch der Königshäuser mit demokratischen Wahlen und einem funktionstüchtigen Parlament durchbrechen. 1849 steigerten sich die Dresdner Unruhen zu mehrtägigen Straßenkämpfen mit Barrikaden, Verletzten und Toten. Zu den berühmtesten damaligen »Revolutionären« (Revolutionssympathisanten) gehörten Richard Wagner und Gottfried Semper. Ihnen gelang die Flucht ins Exil. Andere Aufständische, wie der junge Rechtsanwalt Bernhard Moßdorf und der Nudelfabrikant Anton Bertholdi, wurden zu langjähriger Festungshaft verurteilt. Für beide endete der Gefängnisaufenthalt tödlich. Bei einem ist – nach Zeugenaussagen und gerichtlichen Unterlagen – der Selbstmord gesichert, beim zweiten wurde offiziell der gleiche Grund angegeben. Allerdings gibt es daran begründete Zweifel: Vielleicht wurde er ermordet und die Selbsttötung nur vorgetäuscht.

Als die Barrikadenkämpfe in Dresden 1849 begannen, flüchtete der sächsische König mit seiner Familie auf die Festung Königstein.

Waren dann beide Fraktionen hier oben vertreten? Der König und die gefangenen Unruhestifter?

Bild 4
Zitate aus Gefangenenbriefen und Memoiren, die mit Metallbuchstaben an der Wand angebracht sind. Entwurf des Graphikers Peter Mauksch.

Bild 5
In zwei Medienstationen, eingebaut in einen frei im Raum stehenden Pult-Tisch (Stahlprofile und grau lackiertes Stahlblech), können Besucher mehr Informationen über die fast 1000 Arrestanten, die nachweislich im Laufe der Jahrhunderte auf der Festung inhaftiert waren, nachlesen und recherchieren. Außer Michail Bakunin und August Bebel saßen noch einige Jahre später, genauer gesagt 1899, so berühmte Menschen wie der Dichter Frank Wedekind und der Karikaturist Thomas Theodor Heine auf der Festung als Gefangene. Der Haft- und Strafgrund lautete in beiden Fällen »Majestätsbeleidigung«. Angelika Taube, Andrej Pawluschkow, Alexander Martin und ein Besucher.

Picture 3
The state prison was at its height in the 18th and 19th centuries, which is when the largest number of political prisoners were detained here. They are looked at individually in the second room. On the right-hand wall, which is snow-white and strikingly shows the join with the cross-ridge vaulted ceiling, we displayed a backlit surface with 36 selected portrait photos of prisoners. (Curator: Andrej Pawluschkow.) Some of them spent only a few weeks or months in their cells at the Fortress, whilst others spent years there, and a few were even incarcerated here for life.

Between 1840 and 1850, enlightened citizens of all classes in Dresden were forming a democratic movement – just as they also did in Berlin, and, indeed, across the whole of Europe. They wished to challenge the absolutist powers of the royal houses through democratic elections and a functioning parliament. In 1849, the unrest in Dresden escalated into street battles lasting several days, with barricades and people injured and dead. The most famous »revolutionaries« (revolutionary sympathisers) of the time included Richard Wagner and Gottfried Semper. They successfully fled into exile. Other agitators, such as the young lawyer Bernhard Mossdorf and the noodle manufacturer Anton Bertholdi, were sentenced to several years of imprisonment at the Fortress. For both of them, their time at the Fortress ended with death: one was ascertained to have committed suicide (according to eye-witness accounts and legal documents), and the same cause of death was officially given for the other man. There is, however, reason to doubt this: it is possible he was murdered and his death made to look like a suicide.

When the barricade battles of 1849 began in Dresden, the Saxon king fled with his family to the Königstein Fortress.

Does this mean that both factions were represented here? The king, and the captive agitators?

Picture 4
Quotations from prisoners' letters and memoirs, rendered in metal letters on the wall. Designed by graphic artist Peter Mauksch.

Picture 5
In two media stations, installed in a desk-type table (steel profiles and grey-coated sheet steel), visitors can read about and research the almost 1000 persons who were arrested and who we know were subsequently incarcerated at the Fortress over the centuries. In addition to Michail Bakunin and August Bebel, the Fortress held (a number of years later, in 1899), famous people such as the poet Frank Wedekind and the caricaturist Thomas Theodor Heine. In both cases, the reasons given for the arrest were »*lèse-majesté*«. Angelika Taube, Andrej Pawluschkow, Alexander Martin, and a visitor.

Bild 6
Im Gewölberaum darüber, der nur über eine steile Steintreppe erreichbar ist, haben wir in einer großen Vitrine eine Szene nachgestellt, die sich in einer historischen Wachstube abgespielt haben könnte. (Figuren von Lisa Büscher und Kostüme von Alexandra Hahn.) Über Kopfhörer ist das fiktive Gespräch zwischen den beiden militärischen Bewachern zu hören. (Der Dialog wurde auf der Grundlage eines aktenkundigen Falles vom Kurator der Ausstellung, Andrej Pawluschkow, geschrieben und von Schauspielern eingesprochen.)

Bild 7
Im Außenbereich, genauer gesagt, in einem Torbereich, durch den man von der Johann-Georgenburg über eine steile Treppenanlage direkt zum Medusentor, dem eigentlichen Zu- und Ausgang der Festung, hinuntersteigen kann, gibt es noch einige hinterleuchtete Graphiktafeln zu lesen, die wir – gemeinsam mit dem Graphiker Peter Mauksch – gestaltet haben. Die Texte, geschrieben von dem Kurator Markus Bitterlich, befassen sich ausführlich mit der Geschichte der Johann-Georgenburg. In einer Vitrine ist das Modell der Vorgängerburg aus der frühen Neuzeit zu sehen. Gegenüber hängt ein großer Bildschirm an der Wand, auf dem ein Animationsfilm die Baugeschichte dieses Ortes in ihrer zeitlichen und räumlichen Entwicklung dreidimensional sichtbar und erlebbar macht.

»Zuerst wandte sich der Kurfürst der alten Kaiserburg zu. Unter Beibehaltung der noch aus der Zeit Georgs des Bärtigen stammenden spätgotischen Architekturelemente im Erd- und ersten Obergeschoß ließ er das Gebäude zu einem Jagdschlößchen im Renaissancestil umbauen. Am 27. Juli 1619 fand die feierliche Einweihung in Anwesenheit des Bauherrn, Johann Georgs I., der kurfürstlichen Familie und eines Teils des Hofes, der beiden Baumeister Paul Buchner d. J. und Simon Hoffmann sowie einiger Offiziere der Festung statt. Das Gebäude trägt seitdem den Namen Johann-Georgenburg.« (Angelika Taube.)

Bild 8
2019 wurde auf der Festung das 400jährige Jubiläum des frisch sanierten Gebäudekomplexes gefeiert.

Daß in dem Hauptraum im Erdgeschoß, der zu Mittelalter- und Renaissancezeiten als »Hofestube« benutzt worden war, eine gut erhaltene hölzerne Wäschemangel aus dem 19. Jahrhundert aufgestellt wurde, entspricht nicht der historischen Realität. Sie stand vermutlich dort, wo wir sie vorfanden: in einem Erdgeschoßraum des Torhauses (mit einem separaten Zugang von außen), der heute Teil der Dauerausstellung »In lapide regis« ist. Aber wegen ihres Gewichts und des großen Platzbedarfs während der geplanten Funktionsvorführungen blieb Angelika Taube keine Wahl. Es stand kein anderer leerer Raum dieser Größenordnung mit der erforderlichen Statik auf der Festung zur Verfügung.

Bild 9
Für den vorderen Bereich des jetzigen Mangelraums entwarfen wir ein Holzmöbel mit zwei Sitzen und zwei Virtual-Reality-Brillen. Es soll formal an renaissancezeitliche Fensternischen erinnern. Besucher können sich eine der modernen Brillen, die an dünnen Seilen mit Medienzuleitungen von der eingebauten Holzdecke herabhängen, aufsetzen und virtuell in den historischen Räumen der Johann-Georgenburg spazierengehen. Diener und

festlich im Stil des beginnenden 17. Jahrhunderts gekleidete Gäste schreiten an ihnen vorbei, ganz so, als wären es lebendige Menschen. (Kurator Markus Bitterlich.)

Im ersten, kleineren Ausstellungsraum mit dem gläsernen Windfang wird auf Text- und Medienstelen auf den Bauherrn der Johann-Georgenburg und seine Zeit eingegangen. Im Mittelpunkt: Johann Georg I. mit seiner Frau Magdalena Sibylla. Das Kurfürstenpaar steht in Lebensgröße, gekleidet in prächtige Kostüme, originalgetreu nach einem historischen Gemälde geformt, in einer großen, neu gebauten Vitrine. (Kurator Markus Bitterlich; Gesichter und Körper von Lisa Büscher, Kostüme von Simone Hermsen und Ella Späte, Schmuck von Brit Kolleß und Ella Späte.)

Picture 6
In the vault space above, which can be reached only via a steep stone staircase, we have placed a recreated scene in a large glass case. It is a scene that might have played out in a historic guardroom. (Figures by Lisa Büscher and costumes by Alexandra Hahn.) The fictional dialogue between the two military guards can be listened to through earphones. (This dialogue was created by the curator of the exhibition, Andrej Pawluschkow, based on a documented case, and is spoken by actors.)

Picture 7
In the exterior area – to be precise, in a gate area, through which one could climb down from the Johann Georg Castle via a steep stair directly to the Medusentor (Medusa Gate), the actual point of entrance to and exit from the Fortress, there are some more backlit graphics panels to read, designed by us jointly with the graphic artist Peter Mauksch. The texts, written by curator Markus Bitterlich, provide a detailed history of the Johann Georg Castle. The glass case contains a model of the previous burg from the early modern period. Opposite it, there is a large screen mounted on the wall showing an animated film that allows visitors to see and experience the history of the building work in this place in its three-dimensional expansion through space and through time.

»First, the Prince Elector turned to the old imperial castle. Whilst retaining the late Gothic architectural elements dating from the time of Georg the Bearded on the ground storey and first upper storey, he had the building converted into a small hunting lodge in the Renaissance style. On the 27th of July 1619, it was dedicated with due ceremony and in the presence of the principal, Johann Georg I, the Prince Elector's family and a part of the court, the two master builders Paul Buchner the Younger and Simon Hoffmann and a number of officers of the Fortress. Ever since, the building has borne the name of the Johann Georg Castle.« (Angelika Taube.)

Picture 8
In 2019, celebrations were held at the Fortress to mark the 400-year anniversary of the newly-restored building complex.

In the ground storey's main room (known in mediaeval and Renaissance times as the »court parlour«) is a well preserved wooden washing mangle from the 19th century. This does not correspond to the historical reality. It presumably used to stand where we found it: in a ground storey room of the Gatehouse (with separate access from outside) which is today used for part of the long-term exhibition »In lapide regis«.

However, due to its weight and the amount of space it requires for its function to be demonstrated, Angelika Taube was left with no choice. There was no other empty room of the required dimensions with the necessary stability to be found within the Fortress.

Picture 9
For the forward part of what is now the mangle room, we designed a wooden article of furniture with two seats and with two sets of virtual reality goggles. In shape, it is intended to resemble Renaissance-era window niches. By putting on one of the modern pairs of goggles hanging on thin cables containing media leads from the installed wooden ceiling, visitors can take a virtual walk through the historic spaces of the Johann Georg Castle. Servants and guests dressed for a grand occasion in the style of the early 17th century walk past just as if they were living people. (Curator Markus Bitterlich.)

In the first exhibition room, which is smaller and has a glazed vestibule, there are text and media stelae concerned with the man who commissioned the building of the Johann Georg Castle and his era. In the centre: Johann Georg I with his wife, Magdalena Sibylla. The Prince Elector couple are shown life-size and dressed in grand costumes (faithfully based on a historical painting) in a large, newly built glass case. (Curator: Markus Bitterlich; faces and bodies by Lisa Büscher, costumes by Simone Hermsen and Ella Späte, ornaments by Brit Kolless and Ella Späte.)

1. Die Magdalenenburg von Südwesten.
2. Das große Weinfaß im Keller der Magdalenenburg in einem Kupferstich von M. D. Pöppelmann und L. Zucchi.

1. The Magdalena Castle from the south-west.
2. The large wine barrel in the cellar of the Magdalena Castle in a copper engraving by M. D. Pöppelmann and L. Zucchi.

Riesenweinfaß-Installation im Keller der Magdalenenburg, 2010/11

»Magdalenenburg/Proviantmagazin: 1621/22 als Renaissanceschlößchen erbaut, diente es der Unterbringung des Hofes und als Provianthaus; im Keller von 1725 bis 1819 das 238 000 Liter fassende Weinfaß Augusts des Starken; 1819 Umbau zum bombenfesten Proviantmagazin.« (Angelika Taube.)

Unsere Riesenweinfaß-Installation soll an das einstige Riesenweinfaß erinnern, das 1725 im Auftrag von August dem Starken – als Konkurrenzbau zum »Heidelberger Faß« – in einen der Kellerräume der Magdalenenburg eingebaut worden war. Das Königsteiner Faß, das zwei kleinere Vorgängerfässer hatte, war 11 m hoch und 9,40 m lang. Sein Fassungsvermögen lag 25 000 Liter über dem in Heidelberg. 30 eiserne Reifen hielten die dicken, in Längsrichtung eingebauten Eichenbretter in ihrer runden Faßform.

Auf dem Faß lud eine terrassenartige Plattform mit Brüstung zum Tanzen von maximal 30 Paaren ein.

Im Gegensatz zum Heidelberger Weinfaß, das ziemlich rustikal und schmucklos ausgeführt worden war, prunkte das Königsteiner Faß mit einer reich verzierten Fassade. Im Zentrum saß am unteren Rand ein wohlbeleibter junger, weitgehend nackter Bacchus und begrüßte die Eintretenden mit erhobenem Weinglas. Ob er an den einst berühmten, zwergwüchsigen Hofnarren Perkeo in Heidelberg erinnern sollte, ist unklar.

Da in Sachsen niemand bisher Erfahrungen mit diesen enormen Faßgrößen in dunklen, feuchten Kellern besaß, konnte auch niemand voraussagen, wie lange das Faß, gefüllt mit Wein, dem drohenden Zerfall standhalten würde. Wissen und Erkenntnisse aus dem Bereich des Schiffbaus wären nützlich gewesen, aber bei großen hölzernen Schiffskörpern kam der Wasserdruck ausschließlich von außen und nicht von innen wie hier in Königstein.

Das Königsteiner Faß wurde nur zweimal mit Wein gefüllt. Nach mehr als 40 Jahren zeigten sich die ersten Schäden. Ohne diese schlechte Nachricht nach draußen zu verbreiten, wurde klammheimlich ein zweites, kleineres Faß in den Hohlraum des großen Fasses eingebaut. Die äußere Hülle aus Eichenholz diente nur noch als Attrappe. Aber auch diese Faß-im-Faß-Konstruktion hielt keine 100 Jahre. Das Heidelberger Faß existiert – ungefüllt – noch heute und wird von Touristen »als größtes, hölzernes Weinfaß der Welt« bestaunt, photographiert und über eine Holztreppe betreten.

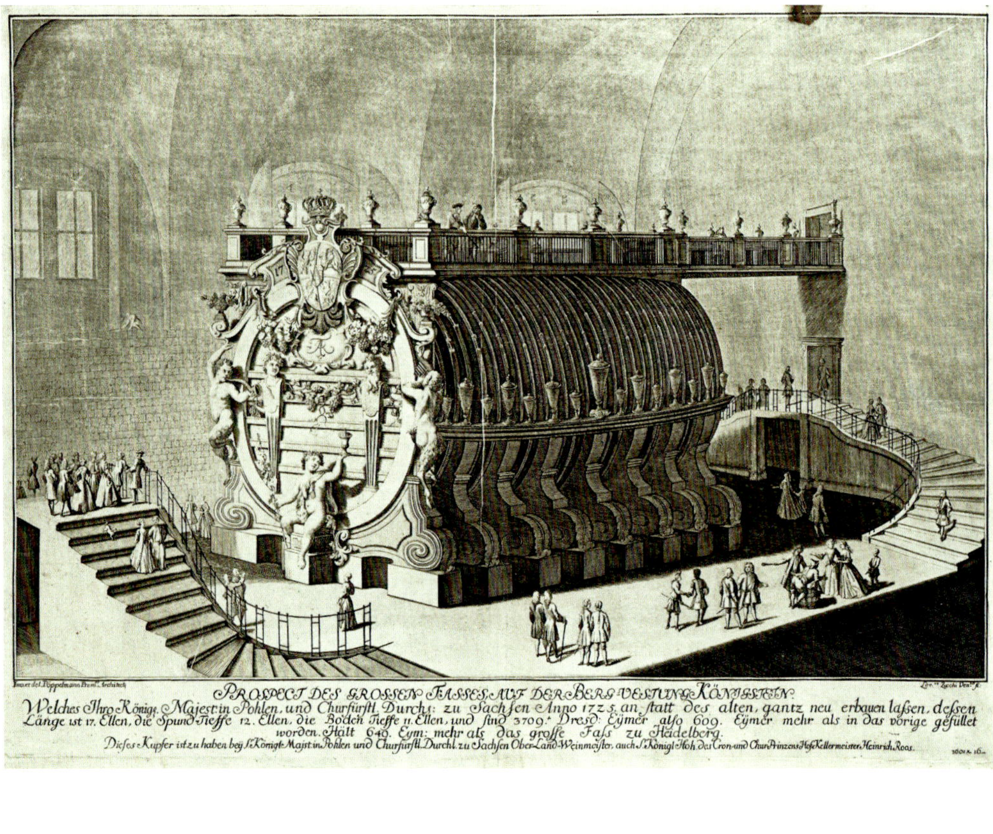

Bild 1
Da der gewölbte Kellerraum in der Magdalenenburg heute – wegen eines gravierenden Umbaus des Gebäudes im 19. Jahrhundert – nur noch halb so hoch ist wie damals, als das »Riesenweinfaß« hier stand, mußte ich mir, nach Beauftragung durch Angelika Taube, etwas ganz Besonderes einfallen lassen. Wir wählten nach langen Entwurfsreihen ein halbes Faß. Es besteht – ähnlich wie ein Schiffsleib, aus senkrecht stehenden, halbrunden Stahlkufen.

Diese Kufen konstruierten wir mehrschichtig und verbanden sie untereinander, so daß drei Lagen normal einfacher, grüner Weinflaschen hintereinander eingefügt werden konnten. Im Gegensatz zum originalen Vorgängerbau ist unser halbes Weinfaß jetzt so transparent wie ein Kirchenfenster. Allerdings fehlte ihm eine innere Lichtquelle. Erst mit dem Einbau einer Beleuchtungsanlage konnten wir die »grüne, trockengelegte Arche Noah« zum Glühen bringen.

Picture 1
Because the vaulted cellar space of the Magdalena Castle is only half as high today as it was when the »giant wine barrel« stood here – owing to a drastic conversion of the building in the 19th century – I had to come up with something quite special when Angelika Taube gave me my task. After a long drafting process, we chose a half-barrel. Similar to the body of a ship, it consisted of vertically standing, semicircular steel runners.

We constructed these runners on multiple levels and connected them in such a way that three layers of normal, simple green wine bottles could be fitted in one behind the other. In contrast to the original construction, our half wine barrel is as transparent as a church window. It did not, however, have an internal light source. It was only after illumination had been installed that we were able to make this »green, dry-docked Noah's Ark« glow.

Giant Wine Barrel installation in the cellar of the Magdalena Castle, 2010/11

»Magdalena Castle/supply depot: built 1621/22 as a small Renaissance palace, it served to accommodate the court and as a storage building; from 1725 to 1819, the cellar contained August the Strong's 238 000 litres wine barrel; in 1819, it was converted into a bombproof supply depot.« (Angelika Taube.)

Our giant wine barrel installation is intended as a reminder of the giant wine barrel of the past, built in 1725 in one of the Magdalena Castle cellars after August the Strong commissioned it to compete with the »Heidelberg barrel«. The Königstein barrel – which was preceded by two smaller barrels, was 11 m high and 9,40 m long. Its capacity was 25,000 litres greater than that of the Heidelberg barrel. 30 iron hoops were used to hold the thick oak boards, which were installed in the longitudinal direction, and to maintain the round shape of the barrel.

On top of the barrel was a wooden terrace-like platform, with balustrades, that up to 30 couples could dance on.

Unlike the Heidelberg wine barrel, which was quite rustic and unadorned in its design, the Königstein barrel had a richly decorated façade. In the centre and at the lower edge, a corpulent, young, and largely naked Bacchus sat, greeting all who entered with a raised wine glass. We do not know for certain whether he is supposed to resemble the famous court fool Perkeo of Heidelberg, who was of dwarf-like stature.

As nobody in Saxony had any previous experience with barrels of such an enormous size in dark and damp cellars, no-one was able to predict how long the barrel, once it was filled with wine, would stave off the threat of decay. Knowledge and experience from the field of shipbuilding would be required, but in the case of large wooden ship hulls, the water pressure is exerted exclusively from the outside, and not from the inside as it is here in Königstein.

The Königstein barrel was only ever filled with wine twice. After more than 40 years, the first signs of damage appeared. This piece of bad news was not shared, and a second, smaller barrel was secretly built into the space inside the large barrel, with the outer oak shell serving only as a dummy. However, this barrel-within-a-barrel construction itself did not last 100 years. The Heidelberg barrel still exists today (unfilled), and is displayed to marvelling tourists as »the biggest wooden wine barrel in the world«. They photograph it and climb onto it by means of a wooden staircase.

Bild 2
Die der heutigen, inneren Zugangstreppe zugewandte Abschlußfront der Rekonstruktion des Riesenweinfasses besteht aus konzentrisch angeordneten, halben Stahlringen. Die Flaschen sind hier so eingebaut, daß die Besucher nur ihre dicken, runden Bodenscheiben sehen. Die eigentlichen Flaschenkörper kann man nur erahnen. In die halbrunden Seitenwangen der liegenden Tonne wurden die leeren Flaschen in drei Schichten hintereinander längs eingebaut, so daß man die Gesamtkörper mit ihrer typischen Flaschenform in der vorderen Schicht gut erkennen kann.

Picture 2
The front termination of the giant wine barrel reconstruction, which is turned towards the internal access stairs of today, consists of concentrically arranged steel half-rings. The bottles are installed here in such a way that the visitors can see only their thick, round bases. We have only a suspicion of the actual bodies of the bottles. In the semicircular side sections of this laid-down barrel, the empty bottles are installed in three layers longitudinally, one behind the other, meaning that one can readily recognise the whole body, with its typical bottle form, in the foremost layer.

Bilder 3–5
Auf der zweiten, dem Eingang abgewandten Frontseite rekonstruierten wir die einstige, reich geschmückte Hauptfassade des Fasses mit einem hinterleuchteten Dia.

Um die sinnliche Wirkung der modernen Kunstinstallation im Sinne der Erinnerung emotional zu steigern, beauftragte Angelika Taube, gemäß meinem Entwurf, den Berliner Komponisten Andreas Lehmann mit einer Ton-Klang-Collage. Ihr Ziel bestand darin, das vergangene 18. Jahrhundert akustisch-atmosphärisch hörbar zu machen. Barockmusik (ein extra für dieses Kunstwerk komponiertes Menuett!), gemischt mit Tanzgeräuschen, Lachen, Gläserklirren und Gesprächsfetzen, geht nach einem Feuerwerk über in heutige Tonbereiche (Rockmusik). Die »Weingeister« werden animiert. Das Riesenweinfaß scheint sich zu erinnern.

Heute ist der Raum nur bei speziellen Führungen – mit Weinausschank – zugänglich.

Für mich gehört diese Installation, die in meinem Büro von Melanie Brugger bearbeitet und – nach Ausschreibung und Vergabe – von den Babelsberger Filmstudios nach unseren Plänen errichtet wurde, zu den wichtigsten modernen Ergänzungsinszenierungen auf der Festung. Leider hielt sich die öffentliche Resonanz – vor allem in den überregionalen Medien – wie bei allen zeitgenössischen Eingriffen und Zutaten in sehr übersichtlichen Grenzen. Trotz manchem kritischen Einwand überwiegt beim Publikum der Wunsch zu ahnen, zu fühlen und zu wissen, »wie es früher einmal war«.

Es bleibt interessant, zu beobachten, wie lange unser Weinfaß aus Stahl und Glas existieren wird. Da es keinem übermäßigem Druck von innen oder außen ausgesetzt ist, bleibt einzig der Staub als dezenter Feind. Aber auch alte Weinkeller mit etwas eingestaubten, manchmal von Spinnweben überzogenen, wertvollen grünen (allerdings: gefüllten) Flaschen haben ihren Charme.

Pictures 3–5

On the second front side, which is turned away from the entrance, we used a backlit diapositive to reconstruct the richly decorated main façade of the wine barrel of yesteryear.

In order to emotionally intensify the sensory effect of this modern art installation in terms of memory, Angelika Taube commissioned the Berlin composer Andreas Lehmann to create a collage of tones and sounds, in accordance with my design. Her goal was to make the bygone 18th century audible, in terms of both acoustics and atmosphere. Baroque music (a minuet composed especially for this artwork!), mixed with the sounds of dancing, laughter, the clinking of glasses and fragments of conversation is followed by a firework and transitions into the sounds of today (rock music). The »wine spirits« become animated. The giant wine barrel appears to remember its old self.

Today, the room is only accessible on special tours – with wine tasting.

I consider this installation, which was developed within my firm by Melanie Brugger and, following a tendering and awarding process, was set up by the Babelsberg film studios according to our plans, to be one of the most significant modern supplementary presentations at the Fortress. Unfortunately, as with all contemporary interventions and additions, the public response has been limited – especially in the media beyond the local region. In spite of a number of objections made by critics, the public overwhelmingly want to get an idea of »how it used to be«, to feel and to know for themselves.

It will be interesting to see how long our wine barrel made from steel and glass exists. As it is not exposed to excessive pressure from inside or outside, its only real enemy is the dust. However, even old wine cellars with rather dusty, even cobwebbed, valuable green bottles have their charm (although these are generally full bottles).

1. Ausstellungsraum in der Magdalenenburg mit temporärem, umgehbarem Spiegelpodest.
2. Der »Spiegelraum« in der Ausstellung »Die sächsische Bastille – Das Staatsgefängnis Festung Königstein 1591 bis 1922« im Torhaus, 2002/03. Die Installation stand als Sinnbild für die höfischen Feste, die im Barock zeitgleich mit der Nutzung der Festung als Staatsgefängnis auf dem Königstein stattfanden.

1. Exhibition room in the Magdalena Castle with temporary, bypassable mirror platform.
2. The »mirror room« in the exhibition »The Saxon Bastille – the Königstein Fortress as a State Prison from 1591 to 1922« in the Gatehouse, 2002/03. The installation stood as a symbol of the courtly festivities that took place on the Königstein in the Baroque period at the same time as the Fortress was used as a state prison.

Spiegelraum, 1998

In den letzten 23 Jahren konnte ich als Gestalter auf der Festung Königstein 12 Wechselausstellungen entwerfen und – gemeinsam mit meinen Mitarbeitern – realisieren. Inhaltlich wurden alle Projekte unter Leitung von Angelika Taube mit ihrem bewährten Wissenschaftler- und Assistententeam erarbeitet. Die Graphik gestaltete Peter Mauksch, die medialen Vertiefungen die Firma Haase & Martin GmbH.

Die erste Wechselausstellung fand ohne Exponate als von mir gestaltete Kunstinstallation 1998 im größeren Ausstellungsraum der Magdalenenburg statt. Um das bereits erwähnte raumgreifende Spiegelpodest herum vollzog sich – eingehüllt in sphärische Klänge – zur Eröffnung eine von Schülerinnen und Schülern der Dresdener Palucca-Schule gestaltete Tanzperformance.

Bevor wir weitere Ausstellungen in der Magdalenenburg einrichten konnten, gab es einige wenige Wechselausstellungen, die im Torhaus gezeigt wurden. Der Raumeinbau in der Ausstellung von 2002/03 über »Die Sächsische Bastille – Das Staatsgefängnis Festung Königstein von 1591 bis 1922« entstand als Nachklang zur Spiegelinstallation in der Magdalenenburg und als Gegenpol zu den Gefangenenschicksalen, um die es in der Ausstellung hauptsächlich ging. Mit Kostümfiguren des Theaterplastikers Christian Paschold ließ ich eine historische Ballszene nachstellen, wie sie vielleicht im Johannissaal zur Zeit des Staatsgefängnisses auf dem Königstein stattgefunden hat. Die gesamte Ausstellung – bis auf die Ballszene – war übrigens vergittert. Die Besucher konnten alle Objekte nur durch das Raster der Gitter sehen. (Kurator: Andrej Pawluschkow.)

Nach den Anfängen im Torhaus wurden wir mehrfach mit der architektonisch-inszenatorischen Gestaltung der Wechselausstellungen im zweiten Obergeschoß der Magdalenenburg beauftragt.

Mirror room, 1998

Over the past 23 years, I have been the designer who created 12 short-term exhibitions at the Königstein Fortress and who implemented them – jointly with my employees. In terms of content, all of the projects were developed under the leadership of managing director Angelika Taube with her proven team of academics and assistants. The graphics were designed by Peter Mauksch, and the enhanced media information by Firma Haase & Martin GmbH.

The first short-term exhibition took place in the larger exhibition room in the Magdalena Castle in 1998 and had no exhibits, being an art installation designed by myself. Around the mirror platform that filled the space, which has been previously mentioned, the opening saw a dance performance by students from Dresden's Palucca School – wrapped in spherical sounds.

Before we were able to set up further exhibitions at the Magdalena Castle, a small number of short-term exhibitions were held in the Gatehouse. The room installation in the exhibition held in 2002/03 on »The Saxon Bastille – the Königstein Fortress as a State Prison from 1591 to 1922« was created as a follow-up to the mirror installation in the Magdalena Castle and as an opposing pole to the fates of the prisoners, with which the exhibition was primarily concerned. Using costumed figures by the theatrical sculptor Christian Paschold, I recreated a historic ball scene, such as might have taken place in the Johannis Hall during the state prison era at the Königstein. The whole exhibition – apart from the ball scene – was, incidentally, behind grids. The visitors could see all of the objects only through the bars of the grates. (Curator: Andrej Pawluschkow.)

After the first activities in the Gatehouse, we were commissioned several times to produce an architectonic/dramaturgical design for the short-term exhibitions on the second upper storey of the Magdalena Castle.

»50 Jahre Museum Festung Königstein – Baustelle zwischen Himmel und Erde«, 2005

Für diese Ausstellung hatte ich ein raumgroßes, in der Mittelachse stehendes, weiß-stilisiertes Baugerüst entworfen, in dem ich die ausgewählten Exponate mit Photos, Plänen und Texttafeln auf verschiedenen Ebenen plazierte. Dazu gab es ein schräges Pult, das sich rings um das Baugerüst an den Außenwänden entlangzog. Hier wurden Gästebücher, Zeitungsartikel, Dokumente und Photos gezeigt. (Kuratorin: Susann Gutsche.)

Die architektonischen Vorgaben für das historische Proviantmagazin, das aus dem Jahr 1819 stammt, waren für die Gestaltung aller Wechselausstellungen prägend.

Wie in den übrigen Hallenbauten auf der Festung bestimmen frei im Raum stehende, kräftige, quadratische Pfeiler (ca. 1 x 1 m) die Raumstruktur: Im größeren Raum gibt es sechs davon, im kleineren, der auch als Veranstaltungssaal benutzt wird, sind es vier. Da große Spannweiten wegen der Holzbalkendecke, die über den weiß verputzten und gestrichenen Kreuzgratgewölben und unter dem Holzfußboden versteckt liegen, nicht möglich waren, sind die freien Raumzonen sehr begrenzt. Ähnlich wie im Neuen Zeughaus haben die Ausstellungsräume in der Magdalenenburg den Charakter von dreischiffigen Hallenkirchen. Daher kommt es, daß auch die Ausstellungsgrundrisse oft axial, rhythmisiert durch die Pfeiler, mit wenig asymmetrischen Störungen gestaltet werden konnten.

Außerdem war es mir nicht immer möglich, freiere, zum jeweiligen Thema passende Inszenierungen – Richtung Szenenbild – zu verwirklichen. Gegenstand der Ausstellungen war in erster Linie die Vermittlung und Veranschaulichung historischer Inhalte, der Festungsgeschichte. Gleichzeitig sollten die Gestaltungen auch ein großes Publikum ansprechen. Angestrebt waren im Durchschnitt 80 000 Besucher pro Sonderausstellung und Jahr. Diese Anzahl wurde manchmal auch weit übertroffen, obwohl ein Ausstellungsraum, der im zweiten Obergeschoß liegt, weniger einladend ist als ein ebenerdiger Raum.

»50 Years of the Königstein Fortress Museum – Construction Site Between Heaven and Earth«, 2005

For this exhibition, I designed a stylised white scaffold to fill the whole room, standing along the central axis. On its various levels, I positioned the selected exhibits: photos, plans, and text panels. There was also an inclined desk that extended along the outer walls, around the scaffolding. Guest books, newspaper articles, documents, and photos were displayed here. (Curator: Susann Gutsche.)

The architectonic specifications for the historic provisions depot, which dates from the year 1819, had an impact on the design of all the short-term exhibitions.

As in the Fortress's other hall constructions, the structure of the room is determined by massive square pillars standing free within the space (approx. 1 x 1 m): there are six of these in the larger room and four in the smaller room, which is also used as an events room. Large span lengths were not possible due to the wood beam ceiling concealed behind the white-plastered and painted cross-ridge vaults and beneath the wood flooring, and this makes the free zones within the room very limited. Similar to the New Armoury, the exhibition rooms in the Magdalena Castle have the character of three-naved hall churches. This is the reason why the exhibition floor plans are often axial, in design with few asymmetrical disruptions, given a rhythm by the pillars.

Additionally, it was not always possible for me to realise more free presentations suited to the theme of each event – in the direction of stage set images. The object of the exhibitions was, principally, the conveying and visualising of historic content: the history of the Fortress. At the same time, the intention was that the designs would appeal to a wide section of the public. The aim was to attract, on average, 80,000 visitors per special exhibition and year. On occasion, this number was greatly exceeded, even though an exhibition space on the second upper storey is less inviting than one at ground level.

1. Skizze zur Wechselausstellung »50 Jahre Museum Festung Königstein«.
2. Das raumbestimmende Ausstellungsgerüst, bestückt mit Objekten, Dokumenten und Bestandsphotos.

1. Sketch of the temporary exhibition »50 Years of the Königstein Fortress Museum«.
2. The space-defining exhibition framework, equipped with objects, documents and stock photos.

Das Brunnenhaus
1 Der alte Lastenaufzug von 1882 wurde zuerst von einer Dampfmaschine und seit 1912 von einem Elektromotor angetrieben. Die Aufnahme entstand kurz vor der Demontage 1978.
2 Von 1967 bis 1972 entstand der neue Personen- und Lastenaufzug. Eingangsbereich um 1970
3 Im Januar 1969 konnte Richtfest gefeiert werden.
4 Bereits im Sommer 1969 erhielt der Aufzug sein Kupferdach. 1972 war es dann soweit. Mit maximal 40 Personen in 80 Sekunden 42 Meter in die Höhe. So leicht und schnell ging es noch nie.
Foto von 1982

»100 Jahre Bergrettung in Sachsen«, 2012
Jubiläumsausstellung der sächsischen Bergrettung

Weil es sich bei diesen Exponaten um keine wertvollen Kunstobjekte, sondern nur um Gebrauchsgegenstände handelte, konnten wir eine größere Inszenierungsgeste wagen. Ich teilte den Raum in zwei Hälften und ließ rechts und links steile Berghänge (aus Holzplatten) errichten. Die Besucher wanderten durch ein stilisiertes Tal. Auf den schrägen, schneeweißen Flächen stellten wir die größeren Rettungsgeräte (Schlitten, Pritschen) ohne Vitrinenhauben aus. Die Pfeiler der Saalarchitektur deuteten wir symbolisch zu Elbsandsteinfelsen um und hängten daran an Seilen Bergretterfiguren auf. Die Kreuzgrat-Gewölbedecke wurde zum symbolischen Himmel über der Szene.

In die hohlen, wie Dachkonstruktionen gebauten, dreieckig-langgezogenen »Landschaftskörper« bauten wir Vitrinen ein, in denen mit gesammelten Objekten der Bergwacht im DRK Landesverband Sachsen e. V. die historische Entwicklung der Bergrettung in Sachsen aus- und dargestellt wurde. Die Besucher sollten sich fühlen wie in stilisierten Höhlen. (Kuratorin: Susann Gutsche.)

»100 Years of Mountain Rescue in Saxony«, 2012
Jubilee exhibition of the Saxon Mountain Rescue Service

Because these exhibits are not valuable art objects but only utilitarian objects, we were able to extend ourselves more in terms of presentation. I divided the room into two halves and set up steep mountainsides (made from wooden panels) on either side. The visitors wandered through a stylised valley. On these sloping, snowwhite surfaces, we set up the larger rescue equipment (sleds, flatbeds) with no glass covers. We treated the pillars of the room's architecture as symbolising Elbe sandstone rocks and suspended figures of mountain rescue personnel from them on cables. The cross ridge vaulted ceiling became a symbolic sky over the scene.

In the hollow elongated triangular »landscape bodies«, which are built like roof constructions, we installed glass cases. These contained collected objects relating to the mountain rescue service in the DRK Landesverband Sachsen e. V., displaying and representing the historic development of mountain rescue operations in Saxony. The intention is that visitors should feel that they are in stylised caves. (Curator: Susann Gutsche.)

1. Blick in den zentralen Ausstellungsbereich, der als Tal geformt war.
2, 3. Vitrinen, die wie Höhlen in das stilisierte Berginnere eingebaut waren.

1. View into the central exhibition area, which was shaped like a valley.
2, 3. Showcases built like caves into the stylised mountain interior.

BERGRETTUNGSWESEN
SACHSEN

»Sachsen und Napoleon – Ein Pakt mit dem Teufel?«, 2013

Ausstellung anläßlich der 200. Wiederkehr des Napoleon-Besuchs auf dem Königstein

Da sich der sächsische Kurfürst und spätere König in der napoleonischen Expansionszeit mit dem selbsternannten Kaiser der Franzosen (im Rheinbund gegen Österreich und Preußen) verbündete, ergaben sich für die Sachsen zuweilen Vorteile, dann wieder Nachteile, besonders stark nach der Völkerschlacht bei Leipzig im Jahr 1813, als der sächsische König in preußische Gefangenschaft geriet und sein Land zuerst unter russische, dann unter preußische Verwaltung gestellt und schließlich territorial gewaltig beschnitten wurde.

Auf den Raumphotos ist zu sehen, daß wir die wichtigsten Gemälde als hinterleuchtete Dias zeigen mußten. Nur wenige Originale konnten ausgeliehen werden. Highlights der Ausstellung waren ein originaler Hut Napoleons aus Paris, sein Sattel und seine Stiefel, die er bei Ausritten in Sachsen getragen hat, und zeitgenössische Waffen.

In der Mitte des Raumes ließen wir eine begehbare Landkarte auf Bodenplatten drucken. (Graphik: Peter Mauksch.) Darauf wurde das Land Sachsen mit seinen Landverlusten nach dem Wiener Kongreß dargestellt. (Kurator: Ingo Busse.)

Napoleon war tatsächlich einmal, 1813, nach seinem fatalen Rußlandfeldzug, auf der Festung Königstein – allerdings zu Fuß und nicht als stürmischer Reiter wie auf dem großen, zentralen Dia, das ihn hoch zu Roß im Gebirge zeigt. Das Originalgemälde aus dem Jahr 1800 stammt von Jacques-Louis David und trägt den Titel *Napoleon Bonaparte beim Überschreiten der Alpen am Großen Sankt Bernhard*. Auf dem Festungsplateau weilte er nur für eine Stunde und genoß den Rundgang mit Fernblick. Ihm gefiel die strategische Lage so gut, daß er gegenüber der Festung, auf der anderen Elbseite, ein großes Feldlager errichten ließ.

»Saxony and Napoleon – A Pact with the Devil?«, 2013

Exhibition on the occasion of the 200th anniversary of Napoleon's visit to the Königstein

The fact that the Saxon Prince Elector, and later King, aligned himself with the self-proclaimed Emperor of France during the period of Napoleonic expansion (in the Rhine Pact against Austria and Prussia), was at times advantageous for Saxony, but then led to disadvantages, particularly after the Battle of the Nations at Leipzig in 1813, when the Saxon king found himself in Prussian captivity while his land was placed first under Russian and then under Prussian administration, finally having its territory severely reduced.

As the photos of the rooms show, we had to present the most important paintings as backlit diapositives. Only a few objects could be loaned. Highlights of the exhibition included an original hat belonging to Napoleon from Paris, his saddle, and his boots, which he rode when riding in Saxony, and contemporary weapons.

For the centre of the room, we had a map printed on floor panels. (Graphics: Peter Mauksch.) It represents the region of Saxony, with its loss of land following the Congress of Vienna. (Curator: Ingo Busse.)

Napoleon did in fact visit the Königstein Fortress in 1813, following his fatal Russian campaign – but on foot, not as the stormy rider shown in the big central diapositive that shows him sitting high on his horse in the mountains. The original painting dating from 1800 was painted by Jacques-Louis David and is entitled *Napoleon Bonaparte crossing the Alps at Great Saint Bernhard*. He only stayed an hour on the Fortress plateau, enjoying the tour and the panoramic view. He was so pleased with the strategic situation that he had a large field camp set up opposite the Fortress, on the Elbe bank.

1, 2. Blicke über die Mittelachse auf eine übergroße, hinterleuchtete Reproduktion von Jacques-Louis Davids Gemälde *Napoleon Bonaparte beim Überschreiten der Alpen am Großen Sankt Bernhard* aus dem Jahr 1800.

1, 2. Views across the central axis of an oversized, backlit reproduction of Jacques-Louis David's 1800 painting *Napoleon Bonaparte Crossing the Alps at the Great Saint Bernard*.

HSEN&
OLEON
EIN P
MIT D
TEUF

»Die Schönste im ganzen Land – Die Festung Königstein im Spiegel der Kunst«, 2014

Da während der Ausstellungsvorbereitung lange nicht klar war, ob es der Geschäftsleitung der Festung Königstein wirklich gelingen würde, die beiden Originale von Canaletto als Leihgabe zu erhalten, spielten diese Bilder während der Gestaltung zunächst eine unsichere Rolle. Daß der Coup am Ende tatsächlich gelang, freute uns alle. Letzter Grund dafür war der Einbau einer Klima- und einer Sicherungsanlage in den größeren Ausstellungsraum der Magdalenenburg.

Die Ausstellungsarchitektur hielt sich zurück. Im Zentrum wurden an zwei separat im Raum stehenden weißen Wänden die beiden berühmten Canaletto-Gemälde präsentiert. Mit einer Absperrung sorgten wir, neben der automatisch-elektronischen Sicherungsanlage und der personellen Bewachung, dafür, daß an den Gemälden kein Schaden entstand. Auch im Bereich der Beleuchtung wurde die neueste Technik angekauft und eingesetzt. Die meisten Besucher waren – laut Gästebuch – stark beeindruckt.

»The Fairest in the Country – The Königstein Fortress in the Mirror of Art«, 2014

While we were preparing for the exhibition, it was unclear for quite some time whether the leadership at the Königstein Fortress would actually succeed in securing the loan of the two original paintings by Canaletto. This meant that the role played by the pictures in the design was initially an uncertain one. We were all delighted when they did in fact succeed in pulling off this coup. The reason for this was, ultimately, the installation of climate control and security systems in the Magdalena Castle's larger exhibition room.

The exhibition architecture was restrained. The two famous Canaletto paintings were presented on white walls in the centre, standing separately within the space. To prevent damage to the painting, we installed a barrier, in addition to surveillance by staff and the automatic electronic security system. The newest technology was likewise purchased and deployed for illumination. To judge by the guestbook, most of the visitors were very favourably impressed.

1. Bernardo Bellotto, genannt Canaletto, *Kommandantengarten und Brunnenhaus auf Festung Königstein*, Öl auf Leinwand, 1756–58. Manchester City Galleries.
2. Bernardo Bellotto, genannt Canaletto, *Magdalenenburg, Brunnenhaus und Johannissaal auf Festung Königstein*, Öl auf Leinwand, 1756–58. Manchester City Galleries.

1. Bernardo Bellotto, called Canaletto, *Commander's Garden and Well House at the Königstein Fortress*, oil on canvas, 1756–58. Manchester City Galleries.
2. Bernardo Bellotto, called Canaletto, *Magdalena Castle, Well House and Johannis Hall at the Königstein Fortress*, oil on canvas, 1756–58. Manchester City Galleries.

»Mönche auf dem Königstein – und wie ›der böse Samen Doctor Luthers‹ sie vertrieb«, 2016
Ausstellung anläßlich des 500. Gründungsjubiläums eines Cölestiner-Klosters auf dem Königstein

Daß auf dem Festungsplateau zu Beginn des 16. Jahrhunderts ein (katholisches) Kloster gegründet wurde, erwähnten wir bereits, genauso wie die Tatsache, daß das Projekt nach acht Jahren, unter dem Einfluß der Reformation, aufgegeben wurde. Der Stifter des zwölfköpfigen Konvents, Herzog Georg der Bärtige von Sachsen, hatte der Neugründung den frommen Namen »Kloster des Lobes der Wunder Mariae« gegeben.

Im Zentrum unserer Klosterausstellung, die von dem Mittelalterhistoriker Markus Bitterlich kuratiert wurde, stand eine originalgroße Nachbildung der einstigen Königsteiner Klosterpforte. Große Teile davon waren Abgüsse des vor etwa 100 Jahren wiederentdeckten Originaltors im Kasemattenbereich der Festung. (Restauratoren: Tina Dömling und Dawid Wardak.) Nach dem Ende der Wechselausstellung wurde das Tor in unsere Dauerausstellung im Torhaus eingebaut. Dort steht es symbolisch für die Übergangszeit von der Burg zur Festung.

Aus dem Kloster mit seinen eigenen Gebäuden auf dem Königstein hat sich – abgesehen von wenigen schriftlichen und gezeichneten Dokumenten – leider so gut wie kein Objekt erhalten.

Ausgestellt waren Originalreliefs, Kapitelle, Säulenfragmente, Madonnenfiguren, Altargerätschaften, Bücher und Flugschriften aus der Reformationszeit. Alle Gemälde, vor allem die Porträts aus dem Umkreis Martin Luthers (von Lucas Cranach) wurden – in Originalgröße – als hinterleuchtete Dias gezeigt.

Emotionaler Höhepunkt dieser Ausstellung war neben dem Klostertor eine Objektinszenierung, die ich im zweiten, nicht immer zur Verfügung stehenden Raum in der Magdalenenburg realisieren konnte. Ich hatte für die Raummitte eine aufrecht stehende, runde, von innen leuchtende Nachbildung einer gotischen Rosette – wie wir sie aus den Westfassaden der Kathedralen in Chartres und Paris kennen – vorgeschlagen. Das im Durchmesser 3,50 m große und 50 cm breite Objekt stand auf einem unbetretbaren, dunkelgrau angestrichenen, 50 cm hohen Sockel mit umlaufendem Geländer und drehte sich permanent den ganzen Tag über langsam um die eigene Achse. Aus versteckten Lautsprechern erklangen Gregorianische Gesänge. Auf einer der Bänke sitzend, die wir im abgedunkelten Raum verteilt hatten, konnten sich die Besucher in eine mittelalterliche, fast mystische Stimmung hineinträumen. Damit begnügten wir uns. Die Reformationsunruhen mit ihren aufrührerischen Predigten, Agitationen, Demonstrationen, Bilderstürmereien, dem Streitgeschrei, dem Kampf- und Kriegslärm sparten wir aus. Durch Luthers Wittenberger Thesenanschlag fand der bisherige, fast tausend Jahre andauernde, etwas weltfremde, zur Religionsdiktatur neigende Traum der katholischen, von Rom aus gesteuerten Kirche ein (teilweises) Ende und spaltete die christliche Welt in zwei sich über Jahrhunderte bekämpfende Fraktionen. Erst in den letzten Jahrzehnten fand im Rahmen der Ökumene eine Annäherung statt.

»The Monks on the Königstein and how they were Driven Away by ›Doctor Luther's Evil Seeds‹«, 2016
Exhibition on the occasion the 500th anniversary of the founding of a Celestine monastery on the Königstein

We have already mentioned that a (Catholic) monastery was founded on the Fortress plateau in the early 16th century, and also that the project was abandoned after eight years owing to the influence of the Reformation. The founder of this twelve-man monastery, Duke Georg the Bearded of Saxony, gave this new foundation the pious name of »Monastery for the Praise of the Miracles of Mary«.

In the centre of our monastery exhibition, curated by mediaeval historian Markus Bitterlich, was an original-size replica of the Königstein monastery portal. Large parts of it were casts taken from the original door, rediscovered around 100 years ago in the casemate area of the Fortress. (Restorers: Tina Dömling and Dawid Wardak.) After the short-term exhibition ended, the portal was integrated into our long-term exhibition in the Gatehouse, where it symbolises the transitional period from castle to fortress.

Unfortunately, apart from a few written and drawn documents, practically no objects remain from this monastery, which had its own buildings at the Königstein.

Exhibits included original reliefs, capitals, column fragments, Madonna figures, altar utensils, books, and pamphlets from the Reformation period. All of the paintings, primarily the portraits of Martin Luther's circle (by Lucas Cranach) were shown in their original size as backlit diapositives.

Aside from the monastery portal, the emotional high point of this exhibition was provided by an object presented by me in the Magdalena Castle second room, which was not always available. For the centre of the room, I proposed an upright, round reproduction of a Gothic rosette that would be lit from within – of the kind we are familiar with from the west façades of the cathedrals of Chartres and Paris. This object was 3.5 m in diameter and 50 cm wide and stood on a pedestal that was 50 cm high and painted dark grey. This pedestal was surrounded by railings, and could not be walked on. Throughout the day, the object would slowly revolve on its axis. Gregorian chants issued from concealed loudspeakers. Visitors could sit on one of the benches provided within this darkened room and enter into a dreamlike mediaeval and almost mystical ambience. We were satisfied with this, and omitted the unrest of the Reformation, with its inflammatory sermons, agitations, demonstrations, acts of iconoclasm, its battle cries, and sounds of war and conflicts. Luther's nailing up of his theses in Wittenberg brought a (partial) end to the dream of a Catholic church controlled from Rome and tending to religious dictatorship, a somewhat unworldly dream that had lasted for almost a thousand years, and fractured the Christian world into two factions that engaged in conflict for centuries. Rapprochement has taken place only in the past few decades, within the framework of ecumenism.

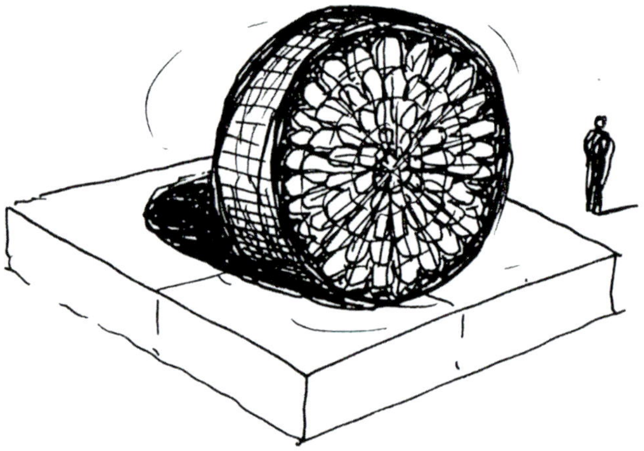

1. Skizze der Nachbildung der Rosette der Kathedrale in Chartres als sich drehendes Rad.
2. Blick in die Ausstellung mit einer Nachbildung des historischen Klostertors.
3. Die Nachbildung der Rosette der Kathedrale Notre Dame in Paris. Während sich das Rosettenrad drehte, waren im Raum Gregorianische Gesänge zu hören.

1. Sketch of the replica of the rose window of the cathedral in Chartres as a rotating wheel.
2. View of the exhibition with a reconstruction of the historic monastery gate.
3. The replica of the rose window of the Notre Dame cathedral in Paris. While the rosette wheel was turning, Gregorian chants could be heard in the room.

Die Menge der Gläubigen aber war ein Herz und eine Seele;
auch nicht einer sagte von seinen Gütern, dass sie sein wären,
sondern es war ihnen alles gemeinsam. (Apg 4,32)
Mönche
auf dem Königstein
The Monks
of Königstein Hill
O mniších
na Königsteinu

»Die Stadtmauer von Nanjing«, 2017

Mit der Ausstellung über Nanjing, die leider wie üblich von den Feuilletons der großen Zeitungen und den Kultursendungen der Fernsehprogramme nicht beachtet wurde, öffnete Angelika Taube den Königsteiner Ausstellungshorizont global. Zum ersten Mal wurde ein Projekt angestoßen, das auf Gegenleistung setzte: Die Festung Königstein sollte 2021 mit einer Ausstellung im neuen City Wall Museum von Nanjing vorgestellt werden. China ist berühmt für die Chinesische Mauer. Daß es dort auch gewaltige, gut erhaltene Stadtmauern und Festungen gibt, ist in Deutschland nicht wirklich bekannt – und das, obwohl die Stadtmauer von Nanjing als eine der größten und am besten erhaltenen in der ganzen Welt gilt.

Uns standen für dieses Projekt in der Magdalenenburg beide Räume zur Verfügung.

Als leuchtender Fluchtpunkt und informative Hauptattraktion wurde am Ende des großen Raumes ein Drohnenfilm an die Wand projiziert, der den aktuellen Zustand der Stadtmauer – meist aus der Vogelperspektive – innerhalb der Millionenstadt Nanjing dokumentiert. Die Stadt ist heute längst über die einstige Mauergrenze hinausgewachsen. Den Film produzierten – nach unseren Vorgaben – die Chinesen selbst.

Im vorderen Raumbereich breiteten wir einen historisch-stilisierten, begehbaren, auf hinterleuchteten Acryltafeln gedruckten Stadtplan am Boden aus, darüber wurde segelartig eine Sternenkarte gespannt. Diese Gegenüberstellung sollte die Theorie zur Stadtgründung Nanjings, wie sie von Guoqing Yang vertreten wird, bildlich darstellen. Er ist der wissenschaftliche Experte für die Stadtmauer in Nanjing. Nach seiner Meinung beruht die Palastgründung, aber auch der nachfolgende Straßen- und Stadtmauerverlauf auf einer bestimmten Sternkonstellation. Nur so konnte – nach Auffassung der alten Chinesen – die Harmonie zwischen Kosmos, Natur, Kaiserpalast, Stadt und den Menschen, die dort leben und wohnen, hergestellt werden. Für uns heute ein Bild, das durch seine Rätselhaftigkeit fasziniert.

Vor den mit rotem, gewelltem Stoff verhängten Außenwänden verteilten wir Stelen, in die Bildschirme eingebaut waren. Darauf konnten die Besucher Photos der Nanjinger Stadtmauer aus dem 19. und 20. Jahrhundert sowie aktuelle Aufnahmen sehen. (Kurator: Markus Bitterlich.)

Der zweite, kleinere Ausstellungsraum wurde in der Mitte, begrenzt durch die vier Pfeiler, von einem roten Mauerblock (gebaut aus Holzplatten) besetzt, in den zwei Großvitrinen und zwei kleinere Vitrinen eingelassen waren. Hier konnten die Besucher die originalgetreu nachgebildeten, sehr wertvollen und damit auch spektakulären Leihgaben aus Nanjing bewundern: ein Kaisergewand, Ritterrüstungen, Waffen (in Originalgrößen und als Modelle), dazu fünf für unsere Verhältnisse übergroße Ziegel mit eingepreßten Herstellerzeichen. Diese Ziegel bestimmen das äußere Erscheinungsbild der Nanjinger Stadtmauer. Die innere, unsichtbare Mauermasse besteht aus Füllmaterial: Lehm, Erde, Sand, Steine, Holz und Bauschutt.

»The City Wall of Nanjing«, 2017

With the exhibition on Nanjing, which, unfortunately, received the usual lack of attention in the culture sections of large newspapers and in the cultural programming of TV broadcasters, Angelika Taube widened the horizons of exhibitions at Königstein to a global level. For the first time, we were embarking upon a project that would involve a reciprocal project: the Königstein Fortress should be presented in an exhibition in the new City Wall Museum in Nanjing in 2021. China is famous for the Great Wall of China. That the nation also has massive and well-preserved city walls and fortresses is a fact that is not widely known within Germany – and this in spite of the city wall of Nanjing being one of the biggest and best-preserved in the whole world. For this project, both of the Magdalena Castle rooms were at our disposal.

As a luminous focal point and informative main attraction, a drone film was projected onto the far end wall of the large room, which documents (largely from a bird's-eye perspective) the current condition of the city wall within Nanjing, a city with a population of millions. The city has long since grown beyond the limits formally imposed by its walls. The film was produced by the Chinese themselves, based on our specifications.

In the front part of the room, we spread a historically-stylised city plan out on the floor, printed on backlit acrylic boards that could be walked on, with a star chart stretched out above it like a sail. This juxtaposition is intended to illustrate the theory of how Nanjing was founded, as advanced by Guoqing Yang. He is the scientific expert for the city wall in Nanjing. In his opinion, the founding of the palace, but also the following course of the streets and of the city wall were determined by a certain constellation of stars. Ancient Chinese beliefs considered this necessary in order to create harmony between the cosmos, nature, the imperial palace, the city, and the people who lived within and inhabited it. For us today, this is a picture, fascinating in its mysteriousness.

In front of the outer walls hung with swagged red fabric, we arranged stelae with screens built into them, on which visitors could view photos of the Nanjing city wall from the 19th and 20th century alongside more recent images. (Curator: Markus Bitterlich.)

In its central zone (delimited by the four pillars), the second, smaller exhibition room was occupied by a red wall block (built from wooden panels), with two large glass cases and two smaller glass cases set into it. Here, visitors could admire faithfully reproduced, extremely valuable and thus also spectacular objects loaned from Nanjing: the robe of an emperor, knights' armour, weapons (in their original size and as models), and five bricks, oversized by our standards, with the manufacturer's symbol pressed into them. These bricks determine the outward appearance of the Nanjing city wall. The internal, non-visible wall mass consists of filler material: loam, earth, sand, stone, wood, and construction rubble.

1. Vitrine mit kleinen Waffenmodellen aus Nanjing.
2. Blick in den Hauptraum der Ausstellung. Auf dem Boden ein historischer Stadtgrundriß von Nanjing. Darüber eine Himmelsdarstellung aus der Zeit der Stadtgründung. Im Fluchtpunkt des Raums war ein Film über die Stadtmauer von Nanjing zu sehen.
3. Vitrine mit der Nachbildung eines historischen Kaisergewands.

1. Display case with small models of weapons from Nanjing.
2. View into the main room of the exhibition. On the floor is a historical ground plan of Nanjing. Above is a sky depiction from the time of the city's foundation. In the vanishing point of the room a film of the Nanjing city wall was shown.
3. Display case with the replica of a historical imperial robe.

»Jugendwerkhof Königstein, 1949–1955«, 2019

Diese Wechselausstellung in beiden Räumen der Magdalenenburg, die sich mit dem Zustand und der Nutzung der Festung Königstein in den Nachkriegsjahren zwischen 1945 und 1955 befaßt, wurde – unter der Leitung von Angelika Taube – von der Kuratorin Maria Pretzschner wissenschaftlich erarbeitet und betreut.

Der Besucherrundweg begann im kleineren Raum mit einer düsteren Ausstellungsinszenierung, die an die schweren Bombenangriffe auf die Stadt Dresden 1944/1945 erinnern sollte. Die Festung Königstein blieb damals zum Glück von Zerstörungen verschont. In Vitrinen und auf einem großen, erhöhten Podest waren Exponate mit authentischen Zerstörungs- und Verbrennungsspuren ausgestellt: verformte Gläser und Flaschen, Bruchstücke von Zaunfeldern und Fassadenschmuck, deformierte Ringanker aus der Kuppel der Frauenkirche, Skulpturenfragmente, eine Nähmaschine und Steine mit schwarzen Brandspuren – Leihgaben des Dresdener Stadtmuseums, die zum Teil in einem speziellen Depot lagern.

Ich ließ auf das rechteckig angeordnete Trümmerfeld Ausschnitte von schwarzweißen Dokumentarfilmen aus den Jahren nach 1945 projizieren. Im Hintergrund der Szene ist ein unscharfes Panoramaphoto der zerstörten Stadt Dresden zu sehen: Ruinen, nichts als Ruinen.

Im zweiten, großen Raum wurde der eigentliche Jugendwerkhof mit Objekten, Dokumenten und Berichten (Hörstationen) von Zeitzeugen visualisiert.

»Von 1949–55 war auf der Festung Königstein ein Jugendwerkhof untergebracht. Jugendwerkhöfe waren Einrichtungen der Jugendhilfe der Deutschen Demokratischen Republik (DDR). Allein in Sachsen gab es Ende des Jahres 1950 zwanzig Jugendwerkhöfe mit ca. 1200 Plätzen. Das Ziel dieser Einrichtungen war es, schwer erziehbare und straffällig gewordene Jugendliche zu ›sozialistischen Persönlichkeiten‹ zu erziehen. Wegen seiner abgeschiedenen Lage galt der Jugendwerkhof Königstein als geschlossener Jugendwerkhof. Hier wurden alle schweren Fälle, die durch die Justiz und die Fürsorge gegangen sind, eingewiesen …« (Maria Pretzschner.)

Vorbild dafür waren die russischen Umerziehungseinrichtungen, die auf der Lehre des Pädagogen Anton Semjonowitsch Makarenko basierten. In der ersten linken Raumnische konnten Besucher auf einer Bank Platz nehmen und Ausschnitte aus dem sehr eindrucksvollen russischen Schwarzweißfilm *Der Weg ins Leben* aus dem Jahr 1931 anschauen. Eine merkwürdige Mischung aus Propaganda, Sozialrealismus und Dokumentarfilm im Stil Sergei Eisensteins.

Danach betrat man den offenen Mittelbereich des Ausstellungsraums. Links und rechts öffneten sich jeweils drei nicht betretbare Konchen. Jede Konche, die man auch als Schau- oder Erinnerungsfenster ohne Gläser betrachten konnte, hatte ihr eigenes Thema: die Anfänge des Jugendwerkhofs Königstein mit Tätigkeiten zur Umgestaltung des Festungsplateaus, politische Erziehung, der Tagesablauf, Schule, Lehrausbildung und Anlerntätigkeiten, besondere Dienste, gelenkte Freizeit und die Auflösung des JWH Königstein.

Vor den Raumbildern mit authentischen Objekten (Schaufeln, Spaten, Schubkarre, Tische, Stühle, Schränke, Werkzeuge) standen – als durchgehendes Band gestaltet – schmale Pultvitrinen. Darin konnten die Besucher gedruckte oder handgeschriebene Dokumente, manchmal auch Photos jener Zeit anschauen und lesen. Jeder der etwa 200 männlichen und weiblichen Insassen erlebte den Jugendwerkhof auf der Festung Königstein anders. Auf einige wirkte der Aufenthalt wie eine harte Gefängniszeit, gesteuert und bewacht von strengen, mehr oder weniger ideologisch bornierten Erziehern und Erzieherinnen. Aber es gab auch Insassen, die positive Erinnerungen daran hatten, vor allem dann, wenn sie aus zerrütteten Familien kamen und im Gegensatz zu ihrem Zuhause hier einen geordneten Alltag erlebten, zu dem auch eine Handwerksausbildung (Schreiner, Schlosser, Gärtner, Maurer) und damit die Vermittlung einer möglichen Perspektive gehörte.

Alle mündlichen Berichte der ehemaligen Insassen entzogen sich einer Ausstellung mit sichtbaren Objekten. Sie waren in Hör- und Medienstationen abrufbar.

Als zentralen Fluchtpunkt des großen Ausstellungsraums wählten wir ein Photo aus, auf dem der Morgenappell zu sehen ist. Einer der Jugendlichen bläst ganz militärisch auf einer Fanfare zum morgendlichen Antreten der Insassen im Freien. In einer Vitrine darunter waren diverse Musikinstrumente ausgestellt, wie sie im Festungsalltag, aber auch bei öffentlichen Auftritten von Schülern und Auszubildenden des Jugendwerkhofs im Ort Königstein eine gewisse Rolle gespielt hatten.

In der Abschluß-Konche des Rundgangs war ein übergroßer Metallschlüssel ausgestellt. Jugendliche der Schlosserwerkstatt hatten ihn zusammengeschweißt und 1955 an den ersten Museumsdirektor übergeben. Er sollte aus der alten Festung mit ihrem wehrhaft-historischen Kern, ihren über Jahrhunderte andauernden Nutzungs- und Bedeutungsmetamorphosen eine DDR-Touristenattraktion mit Museumscharakter formen.

»Juvenile Detention Centre Königstein, 1949–1955«, 2019

This short-term exhibition in the two rooms of the Magdalena Castle, concerned with the situation and the use of the Königstein Fortress in the postwar years between 1945 and 1955, was developed and superintended, in academic terms, by curator Maria Pretzschner – under the leadership of Angelika Taube.

The visitors' tour route began in the smaller room with a dark exhibition presentation reminding of the devastating bombing attacks on the city of Dresden 1944/45. During this time, the Königstein Fortress was fortunately spared from destruction. Exhibits showing authentic traces of destruction and burning were displayed in glass cases and on a large elevated platform: distorted glasses and bottles, fragments of fencing panels and façade decoration, deformed ring beams from the dome of the Frauenkirche, fragments of sculpture, a sewing machine, and stones with black traces of burning – on loan from the Dresden Stadtmuseum. Some of these were stored in a special depositary.

Onto this rectangularly-arranged field of rubble, I projected extracts of black-and-white documentary films from the post-1945 period. In the background of the scene, an out-of-focus panorama photo of the city of Dresden, utterly destroyed, can be seen: ruins, nothing but ruins.

In the second, large space, the actual youth institution was visualised, using objects, documents, and reports (provided at the audio stations) from eye witnesses.

»From 1949–55, a youth institution was housed at the Königstein Fortress. These were youth welfare institutions of the German Democratic Republic (GDR). In Saxony alone, there were twenty youth institutions with approx. 1200 places by the end of the year 1950. The aim of these institutions was to educate difficult youths in trouble with the law into ›socialist personalities‹. Due to its remote location, the Königstein youth institution was considered a closed youth institution. All the difficult cases who had been through the justice and care systems were assigned here …« (Maria Pretzschner.)

It was modelled on the Russian re-education institution based on the doctrines of the educationalist Anton Semyonovich Makarenko. On the first room niche on the left, visitors could take a seat on a bench and view extracts from the 1931 Russian black-and-white film *Road to Life*, which makes a great impression: a curious mix of propaganda, social realism, and documentary film in the style of Sergei Eisenstein.

After this, one entered the open central area of the exhibition space. Conch spaces opened up, which cannot be entered: three on the left, three on the right. Each conch, which might be regarded as a glassless display window or a window of memory, had its own theme: the beginnings of the Königstein youth institutions with activities for the redesign of the Fortress plateau, political education, the rhythm of the day, school, apprenticeship training and practical activities, special commissions, controlled leisure time, and the dissolution of the JWH Königstein.

In front of the room images with authentic objects, (shovels, spades, a wheelbarrow, tables, chairs, cabinets, tools) narrow desk glass cases were arranged, running as a continuous band. In these glass cases, visitors could look at and read printed and hand-written documents and sometimes also photos from this period. Each of the inmates – around 200, both male and female – had a different experience of the youth institution at the Königstein Fortress. Some found their stay to be like a hard term in prison, controlled and under constant surveillance by educators with a narrow ideological mindset. However, there are also former inmates who have positive memories, particularly those who came from troubled families and had their first experience of an ordered day-to-day life here that was denied to them in their own homes, with the added possibility of learning a trade (carpenters, locksmiths, gardeners, bricklayers) and thus prospects for the future.

All of the verbal reports from former inmates were taken from an exhibition with visible objects. One could access them from audio and media stations.

As the central point of focus for the big exhibition space, we chose a photo that shows morning roll call. One of the youths is blowing, in military style, a fanfare for the morning assembly of the inmates outside the buildings. In a glass case beneath, various musical instruments were exhibited; these would have played a certain role both in day-to-day life at the Fortress and in public appearances by the students and trainees at this residential youth institution in the locality of Königstein.

In the final conch-form space of the tour, an oversized metal key was exhibited. The young people of the metalwork workshop welded it together as a gift to the first museum director in 1955. He was to make the old Fortress – with its historic defensive core, its metamorphosis of use and significance over the centuries – into a GDR tourist attraction with the character of a museum.

1, 2. Vitrinen-Nischen im Hauptausstellungsraum. Gezeigt wurden hier Gerätschaften, die von den Jugendwerkhof-Insassen benutzt und teilweise selbst von ihnen hergestellt worden waren.

1, 2. Display case niches in the main exhibition room. On display were tools that had been used by the inmates of the Juvenile Detention Centre, some of which they had made themselves.

3. Blick in den ersten Raum der Ausstellung. Zu sehen war hier eine Reminiszenz an die Kriegszerstörung Dresdens mit einer Filmprojektion auf originale Trümmerstücke aus jener Zeit.
4. Schlußnische mit einem Riesenschlüssel, der von Jugendwerkhof-Insassen bei der Auflösung der Einrichtung an die neue Leitung übergeben wurde.

3. View into the first room of the exhibition. On display was a reminiscence of the war destruction of Dresden with a film projection on original debris from that time.
4. Final niche with a giant key, which was handed over to the new management by inmates of the Juvenile Detention Centre when the institution was dissolved.

»Hohe Gäste auf Sachsens schönster Feste«, 2020

Bei unserer Ausstellung über »hohe Gäste« griffen wir auf die klassische Konchengliederung, wie man sie aus alten Museen kennt, zurück. An den dunkelgrün gestrichenen Wänden waren vor allem goldgerahmte Ölgemälde mit Porträts von adeligen Besuchern, aber auch von Künstlern und Wissenschaftlern des 18. und 19. Jahrhunderts zu sehen. Sie alle hatten die Festung als »hohe Gäste«, von Berufs wegen oder als frühe Touristen besucht.

Leider wurde die ursprüngliche Idee, die »Hohen Gäste« mit der touristischen Entwicklung des Elbsandsteingebirges und der Festung Königstein zu verknüpfen, frühzeitig aufgegeben. Bereits Mitte des 19. Jahrhunderts gab es einen regen Dampfschiffahrtsverkehr zwischen Dresden, Pirna, Königstein und Bad Schandau. Die Schiffe mußten auch gegen die Strömung fahren können. Aber erst mit dem Bau einer Bahntrasse entlang der Elbe und mit der Errichtung vieler kleiner Bahnhöfe – so auch im Ort Königstein – begann der bürgerliche Ausflugsverkehr in dieser romantischen Gegend wirklich aufzublühen. Vom Königsteiner Bahnhof konnte man zu Fuß auf die Festung hochwandern oder sich von einer Pferdekutsche bis zum Haupteingang fahren lassen. Der Gedanke, eine Zahnradbahn oder eine Seilbahn zu bauen, ist damals noch nicht aktuell gewesen, denn der Königstein war weiterhin – bis 1913 – eine Festung im militärischen Sinne und deshalb nur in Friedenszeiten für touristische Besucher zugänglich. Erst ein in den Fels eingebauter Aufzug vom oberen Parkplatz hinauf zum eigentlichen Festungsplateau brachte etwas Erleichterung vor allem für ältere Menschen. Aber zu diesem Fortschritt kam es erst während der DDR-Zeit.

»Important Guests at Saxony's Most Beautiful Fortress«, 2020

For our exhibition on »important guests«, we made use of the classical conch structure, well-known from old museums. On the dark-green-painted walls, primarily gold-framed oil portraits of noble visitors were displayed, but also of artists and scientists of the 18th and 19th century. All of them visited the Fortress as »important guests«, either professionally or as early tourists.

Unfortunately, the original idea of connecting the »illustrious guests« with tourism development in the Elbe sandstone mountains and the Königstein Fortress had to be given up at an early stage. By the mid-19th century, brisk steamship traffic existed between Dresden, Pirna, Königstein, and Bad Schandau. These ships also had to travel against the current. However, the flow of middle-class tourists on daytrips to this romantic area did not truly begin to blossom until after the construction of a railway along the Elbe and the setting up of many small stations – including in the locality of Königstein. From the station at Königstein, one could walk to the Fortress on foot, or take a horse-drawn carriage up to the main entrance. The notion of building a rack-and-pinion railway or cable car system was not realised at the time, as the Königstein remained a military fortress until 1913, and was thus accessible to tourist visitors only during peacetime. Not until a lift was installed to take people from the upper car park to the actual Fortress plateau was some relief afforded, especially to older people. This advancement, however, did not occur until the GDR period.

1. An den Wänden hingen fast nur originale Ölgemälde aus verschiedenen Jahrhunderten.
2. Die legendäre Personenwaage aus historischen Zeiten. Fürstliche Gäste wurden damit zum Spaß vor und nach dem Essen gewogen.
3. Bis 1915 sind Besuche der Wettiner auf dem Königstein nachweisbar. Links Gemälde von König Albert und seiner Gattin Königin Carola. Bei ihrer Ankunft auf der Festung am 7. Oktober 1874 wurden 33 Salutschüsse abgefeuert. Beim ersten Schuß mußte die sächsische Flagge gehißt werden. Rechts ein Gemälde des letzten sächsischen Königs, Friedrich August III.

1. On the walls hung almost only original oil paintings from different centuries.
2. The legendary personal scales from historical times. Princely guests were weighed with it for fun before and after the meal.
3. There is evidence of visits by the Wettins to Königstein until 1915. On the left, paintings of King Albert and his wife Queen Carola. On their arrival at the Fortress on 7 October 1874, 33 gun salutes were fired. At the first shot the Saxon flag had to be hoisted. On the right a painting of the last Saxon king, Friedrich August III.

in Vorwissen
werden.«
en von Geyer, 10. Juni 1769
Die Gouverneure von Dresden
Öffentliches Wiegen – ein fürstliches Vergnügen

»Bei der Ankunft Sr. Majestät
am Brunnenhause brachte der Zeug-Feldwebel Stephan ein 'Hoch' aus.«
Chronik der Festung Königstein, 7. Oktober 1874

»Viel früher als gedacht! – Der Königstein in der Bronzezeit«, 2021

Der Schlüsseltext zu dieser Wechselausstellung lautet: »Jungbronzezeitliche Scherben, 1200–1050 v. Chr. Diese Scherben entdeckten Archäologen 2016 bei Tiefbauarbeiten am Artillerieschuppen auf dem südöstlichen Plateau des Königsteins. Sie befanden sich mit etwa 50 weiteren Bruchstücken von Tongefäßen in einer unversehrten Abfallgrube. Der Fund belegt eine Besiedlung des Königsteins in der Jungbronzezeit. Eine Scherbe fällt durch ihre Gestaltung besonders auf. Sie gehörte zu einem großen Vorratsgefäß, dessen Halsansatz eine Leiste mit Fingereindrücken zierte.« (Kuratoren: Robert Dietze und Markus Bitterlich.)

»Much earlier than Imagined! – The Königstein Hill in the Bronze Age«, 2021

The key text for this short-term exhibition is: »Late Bronze Age shards, 1200–1050 BC. These shards were discovered by archaeologists in 2016 during excavation works at the artillery shed on the south-east plateau of the Königstein. They were found in an untouched refuse pit, along with around 50 further fragments of clay vessels. This find proves that the Königstein was inhabited during the early Bronze Age. One shard has a particularly striking design. It was once part of a big storage vessel with the base of neck decorated with a strip featuring fingerprints.« (Curators: Robert Dietze and Markus Bitterlich.)

1. Zentraler Blick in die Ausstellung über bronzezeitliche Funde aus der näheren und weiteren Umgebung.

1. Central view of the exhibition on Bronze Age finds from the nearer and more distant surroundings.

Der Königstein
in der europäischen Geschichte

2. Entwurfsskizze zur Ausstellung.
3. In einer größeren Vitrine wurde ein Vorratsgefäß aus Keramik ausgestellt, das von Archäologen und Restauratoren aus bronzezeitlichen Scherben zusammengesetzt worden war.
4. Nachbau eines bronzezeitlichen Webstuhls. Im Hintergrund Fragmente eines Lehmwand-Winkels und eines Landschaftsmodells mit bronze-zeitlicher Siedlung.

2. Design sketch for the exhibition.
3. In a larger display case, a storage vessel from ceramics was exhibited, which had been assembled from Bronze Age shards by archaeologists and restorers.
4. Replica of a Bronze Age loom. In the background, fragments of a clay-wall angle and a landscape model with a Bronze Age settlement.

»Zwischen Möhrenbeet und Tarnbepflanzung – Facetten des Festungsgrüns auf dem Königstein«, 2022

Im Einführungstext der Hauptkuratorin dieser Ausstellung, Stefanie Krihning (sie arbeitet an dem Projekt gemeinsam mit Maria Pretzschner), heißt es: »Die Festung Königstein besteht nicht nur aus Mauern und Gebäuden, das Plateau des Sandsteintafelberges war immer auch mit Vegetation bewachsen ..., der Königstein ist seit Jahrhunderten Wohnort von Menschen, die den Ort ihren Bedürfnissen anpassten; in den letzten 500 Jahren waren dies im wesentlichen: Selbstversorgung mit Nahrungsmitteln, Sicherheit und Verteidigung, Schönheit und Repräsentation.«

»Between Carrot Beds and Camouflage Planting – Facets of the Fortress Greenery on the Königstein«, 2022

The introductory text by this exhibition's chief curator Stefanie Krihning (working on the project jointly with Maria Pretzschner) states it as follows: »The Königstein Fortress consists of more than just walls and buildings; the plateau of the sandstone flat-topped mountain was always covered with vegetation ..., the Königstein has been inhabited by human beings for centuries, who have adapted the place to their needs; in the past 500 years, these needs have been largely the provision of foodstuffs, security and defence, beauty and representation.«

1. Entwurfsskizze zur geplanten Ausstellung über das Festungsgrün auf dem Königstein im Laufe der Jahrhunderte. Im Titel »Zwischen Möhrenbeet und Tarnbepflanzung« läßt sich die ganze Bandbreite der gärtnerischen und militärischen Ziele ablesen.

1. Draft sketch of the planned exhibition about the Fortress greenery on the Königstein over the centuries. The title »Between Carrot Bed and Camouflage Planting« shows the whole range of horticultural and military planning objectives.

Liste der Mitwirkenden

Wer übersehen oder vergessen wurde, möge mir diesen Fehler verzeihen.

»In lapide regis – Auf dem Stein des Königs«
Architektur: Sanierung und Modernisierung des Torhauses und der Streichwehr unter der Gesamtleitung des Staatsbetriebs Sächsisches Immobilien- und Baumanagement, kurz SIB, Niederlassung Dresden I
Entwurf, Planung: Springer Architekten, Berlin, unter der Mitwirkung des Landesamts für Denkmalpflege Sachsen
Historische Bauuntersuchung: Hartmut Olbrich
Restaurierungen: Tina Dömling und Dawid Wardak
Lichtplanung: studio dinnebier
Gesamtleitung der neuen Dauerausstellung: Angelika Taube, Geschäftsführerin der Festung Königstein gGmbH
Assistenz: Jenni Schwan
Historiker, Museologen, Kuratoren: Markus Bitterlich, Andrej Pawluschkow, Ingo Busse
Museumspädagogik: Maria Pretzschner
Technische Leitung: Hardy Hochgräf
Entwurf, Planung, Ausschreibung und Bauleitung der neuen Dauerausstellung: Hans Dieter Schaal
Detailplanung und Bauleitung im Büro Schaal: Melanie Brugger
Figuren: Lisa Büscher und Alexandra Hahn
Dioramen: Paul Wells und Sarah Hendry
Modelle: Ulrich Haselhuhn, Bernhard Sorg, Burkard Hauck, Modellbau Milde
Museumspädagogische Stationen: Molitor GmbH Berlin, Axel Bierwolf, Bernhard Sorg, Björn Hacker, Steve Viezenz, Björn Grunau, Lutz Stützner
Graphik: Peter Mauksch
Graphikproduktion: Werbemittel Werner Trache
Medien: Haase & Martin GmbH
Filme: ArcTron 3D GmbH, René Micknaß, Axel Weckschmied, Ernst Hirsch
Hörstationen: herold media
Musik: Peter A. Bauer, Dresdner Barockorchester, Kinderchor der Sächsischen Staatsoper Dresden unter der Leitung von Andreas Heinze, David Rotter
Ausführende Baufirma: Heinzelmann GmbH
Vitrinenbau: Sehner GmbH
Malerarbeiten: Christian Kotte, Veit Lehmann
Raumeinrichtung: Steffen Dietz, Reichelt die Einrichter OHG
Exponateinrichtung: Fißler & Kollegen GmbH

Altes Zeughaus
Sanierung und Modernisierung: unter der Leitung des SIB, Niederlassung Dresden I
Örtliche Planung und Bauleitung: Evelyn Baumann, Dohma
Projektleitung der neuen Dauerausstellung: Angelika Taube
Assistenz: Jenni Schwan
Wissenschaftliche Kuratoren: Ingo Busse und Thoralf Rauchfuß; Teilbereich Pädagogik: Maria Pretzschner
Technische Leitung: Hardy Hochgräf
Ausstellungsplanung: Hans Dieter Schaal
Detailplanung und Bauleitung im Büro von Hans Dieter Schaal: Armin Teufel
Graphik: Peter Mauksch
Graphikproduktion: Werbemittel Werner Trache
Medien: Haase & Martin GmbH, Biermann-Jung Kommunikation und Film
Modell: Paul Wells
Ausführende Baufirma: Sehner GmbH
Exponateinrichtung: Fißler und Kollegen GmbH

Neues Zeughaus
Sanierung und Modernisierung des Gebäudes: SIB, Niederlassung Dresden I, nach Vorgaben des Berliner Architekturbüros Heidenreich & Springer
Beleuchtung: studio dinnebier
Wissenschaftliche Leitung: Gorch Pieken (damals wissenschaftlicher Direktor des MHM, Militärhistorisches Museum, Dresden)
Ausstellungsentwurf: Hans Dieter Schaal mit Armin Teufel und Christin Seifert
Detailplanung, Ausschreibung und Bauleitung: Schubert & Horst
Projektleitung: Falk Lukesch
Graphik: Katrin Miklich
Medien: MHM, Dresden
Restaurierung und Klimaschutz: Lutz Strobach (MHM)
Herstellende Firma: Seiwo-Technik; der Mittelalter-Ritter auf der linken Plattform: Firma Freyhand; Plattner: René Kohlstruck, Hamburg
Alle Exponate sind im Besitz des Dresdner MHM.

Brunnenhaus
Sanierung: durch das SIB, Niederlassung Dresden I
Projektleitung der Ausstellung: Angelika Taube
Kurator: Ingo Busse
Technische Leitung: Hardy Hochgräf
Entwurf und Planung der Ausstellung: Hans Dieter Schaal
Konstruktionsplanung und Bauleitung im Büro Schaal: Armin Teufel
Bau: Heinzelmann GmbH
Vitrinen: Sehner GmbH
Medientechnik: Ingenieurbüro Steffen Dreßler (Planung) und MediaTronic GmbH (Ausführung)
Filme: Biermann-Jung Kommunikation und Film (Brunnenbefahrung) und Lutz Stützner (Animation)
Modelle: Paul Wells, London, und Designprojekt GmbH
Graphik: Peter Mauksch
Graphikproduktion: Werbemittel Werner Trache
Modellbau: Bernd Naguschewski

Johann-Georgenburg
Sanierung und Modernisierung: SIB, Niederlassung Dresden I, nach Plänen und Vorgaben der Architektengemeinschaft Milde + Möser, Pirna
Projektleitung der Ausstellung: Angelika Taube
Kuratoren: Markus Bitterlich, Andrej Pawluschkow und Ingo Busse
Technische Leitung: Hardy Hochgräf
Ausstellungsgestaltung: Hans Dieter Schaal
Detailplanung und Bauleitung im Büro Schaal: Armin Teufel
Bau: AMF Theaterbauten GmbH
Graphik: Peter Mauksch
Graphikproduktion: Werbemittel Werner Trache
Medien: Haase & Martin GmbH, ArcTron 3D GmbH, Biermann-Jung Kommunikation und Film, herold media
Modell: Ulrich Haselhuhn
Vitrinen: Sehner GmbH
Figuren (Wachstube): Gesichter und Körper von Lisa Büscher
Kostüme: Alexandra Hahn, Simone Hermsen und Ella Späte
Schmuck: Brit Kolleß und Ella Späte

Riesenweinfaß-Installation
Sanierung des Gebäudes: SIB, Niederlassung Dresden, nach Plänen von F29-Architekten, Peter Zirkel
Anregung und Gesamtleitung: Angelika Taube
Idee und Planung: Hans Dieter Schaal
Detailplanung und Bauleitung: Melanie Brugger im Architekturbüro Schaal
Ausführende Firma: Studio Babelsberg
Graphik: Peter Mauksch
Komposition der Klanginstallation: Andreas Lehmann

Wechselausstellungen
Gesamtleitung bei allen zwölf temporären Ausstellungsprojekten: Angelika Taube
Wissenschaftliche Kuratoren: Ingo Busse, Andrej Pawluschkow, Susann Gutsche, Markus Bitterlich und Maria Pretzschner; bei manchen Projekten wurden frei arbeitende Wissenschaftler dazu engagiert: Robert Dietze, Stefanie Krihning
Graphik: Peter Mauksch
Graphikproduktion: Werbemittel Werner Trache
Medien: Haase & Martin GmbH
Bau: Walther GmbH, AMF-Theaterbauten, Heinzelmann GmbH

Literatur zur Festung Königstein

Angelika Taube, *Festung Königstein*. Edition Leipzig 2014.
In Lapide Regis – Auf dem Stein des Königs. Katalogbuch zur Dauerausstellung über die Geschichte des Königsteins, herausgegeben von der Festung Königstein gGmbH unter Leitung von Angelika Taube. Beiträge von den Kuratoren der Ausstellung und verschiedenen Wissenschaftsautoren. Festung Königstein 2017.

Zu manchen Wechselausstellungen erschienen kleinere Katalogbände oder Begleithefte, so etwa
Die Schönste im ganzen Land. Die Festung Königstein im Spiegel der Kunst. Festung Königstein 2014.
Das Kloster des Lobes der Wunder Mariae auf dem Königstein. Festung Königstein 2016.
Jugendwerkhof Königstein 1949–1955. Festung Königstein 2019.
Hohe Gäste auf Sachsens schönster Feste. Festung Königstein 2020.
Viel früher als gedacht! Der Königstein in der Bronzezeit. Festung Königstein 2021.

List of those involved in the projects

If I have forgotten or overlooked anyone, I hope he or she will forgive me.

»In lapide regis – On the Stone of the King«

Architecture: restoration and modernisation of the Gatehouse and the close-range defence under the general leadership of the state-run concern Sächsisches Immobilien- und Baumanagement, abbreviated to SIB, Dresden I branch
Design, planning: Springer Architekten, Berlin, assisted by the Landesamt für Denkmalpflege Sachsen (the regional authority for monument preservation, Saxony)
Historical building assessment: Hartmut Olbrich
Restorations: Tina Dömling and Dawid Wardak
Lighting planning: studio dinnebier
Overall management of the new long-term exhibition: Angelika Taube, managing director of Festung Königstein gGmbH
Assistant: Jenni Schwan
Historians, museologists, curators: Markus Bitterlich, Andrej Pawluschkow, Ingo Busse
Museum education: Maria Pretzschner
Technical management: Hardy Hochgräf
Design, planning, tendering and construction management for the new long-term exhibition: Hans Dieter Schaal
Detail planning and construction management at Büro Schaal: Melanie Brugger
Figures: Lisa Büscher and Alexandra Hahn
Dioramas: Paul Wells and Sarah Hendry
Models: Ulrich Haselhuhn, Bernhard Sorg, Burkard Hauck, Modellbau Milde
Museum educational stations: Molitor GmbH Berlin, Axel Bierwolf, Bernhard Sorg, Björn Hacker, Steve Viezenz, Björn Grunau, Lutz Stützner
Graphics: Peter Mauksch
Graphic production: Werbemittel Werner Trache
Media: Haase & Martin GmbH
Films: ArcTron 3D GmbH, René Micknass, and Axel Weckschmied, Ernst Hirsch
Listening stations: herold media
Music: Peter A. Bauer, the Dresden Baroque Orchestra, the children's choir of the Saxon State Opera Dresden directed by Andreas Heinze, David Rotter
Implementing construction firm: Heinzelmann GmbH
Glass case construction: Sehner GmbH
Painting works: Christian Kotte, Veit Lehmann
Setting up of room: Steffen Dietz, Reichelt die Einrichter OHG
Setting up of exhibits: Kollege Fissler GmbH

Old Armory

Restoration and modernisation: under the leadership of the SIB, Dresden I branch
Local planning and construction management: Evelyn Baumann, Dohma
Project head for the new long-term exhibition: Angelika Taube
Assistant: Jenni Schwan
Academic curators: Ingo Busse and Thoralf Rauchfuss; educational section: Maria Pretzschner
Technical management: Hardy Hochgräf
Exhibition planning: Hans Dieter Schaal
Detail planning and construction management within the firm of Hans Dieter Schaal: Armin Teufel
Graphics: Peter Mauksch
Graphic production: Werbemittel Werner Trache
Media: Haase & Martin GmbH, Biermann-Jung Kommunikation und Film
Model: Paul Wells
Implementing construction firm: Sehner GmbH
Setting up of exhibits: Fissler und Kollegen GmbH

New Armoury

Restoration and modernising of the building: SIB, Dresden I branch, based on the specifications of the Berlin architecture firm of Heidenreich & Springer
Illumination: studio dinnebier
Scientific direction: Gorch Pieken (at that time scientific director of the MHM, Militärhistorisches Museum, Dresden)
Exhibition design: Hans Dieter Schaal with Armin Teufel and Christin Seifert
Detail planning, tendering and construction management: Schubert & Horst
Project director: Falk Lukesch
Graphics: Katrin Miklich
Media: MHM, Dresden
Restoration and climate protection: Lutz Strobach (MHM)
Manufacturing firm: Seiwo-Technik, the mediaeval knight on the left-hand platform: Firma Freyhand; plate armourer: René Kohlstruck, Hamburg
All of the exhibits are the property of the Dresden MHM.

Well House

Restoration: by the SIB, Dresden I branch
Head of project for the exhibition: Angelika Taube
Curator: Ingo Busse
Technical management: Hardy Hochgräf
Exhibition design and planning: Hans Dieter Schaal
Construction planning and construction management at Büro Schaal: Armin Teufel
Construction: Heinzelmann GmbH
Glass cases: Sehner GmbH
Media technology: Ingenieurbüro Steffen Dressler (planning) and MediaTronic GmbH (implementation)
Films: Biermann-Jung Kommunikation und Film (well inspection) and Lutz Stützner (animation)
Models: Paul Wells, London, and Designprojekt GmbH
Graphics: Peter Mauksch
Graphic production: Werbemittel Werner Trache
Model making: Bernd Naguschewski

Johann Georg Castle

Restoration and modernisation: SIB, Dresden I branch, based on plans and specifications by the architecture collective Milde + Möser, Pirna
Project management of the exhibition: Angelika Taube
Curators: Markus Bitterlich, Andrej Pawluschkow and Ingo Busse
Technical management: Hardy Hochgräf
Exhibition design: Hans Dieter Schaal
Detail planning and construction management at Büro Schaal: Armin Teufel
Construction: AMF Theaterbauten GmbH
Graphics: Peter Mauksch
Graphic production: Werbemittel Werner Trache
Media: Haase & Martin GmbH, ArcTron 3D GmbH, Biermann-Jung Kommunikation und Film, herold media
Model: Ulrich Haselhuhn
Glass cases: Sehner GmbH
Figures (guardroom): faces and bodies by Lisa Büscher
Costumes: Alexandra Hahn, Simone Hermsen, and Ella Späte
Adornment: Brit Kolless and Ella Späte

Giant Wine Barrel installation

Restoration of the building: SIB, Dresden I branch, based on plans by F29-Architekten, Peter Zirkel
Initiative and overall leadership: Angelika Taube
Idea and planning: Hans Dieter Schaal
Detailed planning and direction of construction: Melanie Brugger at Architekturbüro Schaal
Implementing firm: Studio Babelsberg
Graphics: Peter Mauksch
Composition of sound installation: Andreas Lehmann

Short-term exhibitions

Overall direction of all twelve temporary exhibition projects: Angelika Taube
Academic curators: Ingo Busse, Andrej Pawluschkow, Susann Gutsche, Markus Bitterlich, and Maria Pretzschner. Independent academics were employed for a number of projects: Robert Dietze, Stefanie Krihning
Graphics: Peter Mauksch.
Graphic production: Werbemittel Werner Trache
Media: Haase & Martin GmbH
Construction: Walther GmbH, AMF-Theaterbauten, Heinzelmann GmbH

Literature on the Königstein Fortress

Angelika Taube, *Festung Königstein*. Edition Leipzig, 2014.
In Lapide Regis – Auf dem Stein des Königs. This is the catalogue book for the long-term exhibition on the history of the Königstein, issued by the Festung Königstein gGmbH under the leadership of Angelika Taube. It contains contributions from the exhibitions' curators and from various academic authors. Festung Königstein, 2017.

Smaller catalogue volumes or accompanying booklets have been produced for some short-term exhibitions, such as
Die Schönste im ganzen Land. Die Festung Königstein im Spiegel der Kunst. Festung Königstein, 2014.
Das Kloster des Lobes der Wunder Mariae auf dem Königstein. Festung Königstein, 2016.
Jugendwerkhof Königstein 1949–1955. Festung Königstein, 2019.
Hohe Gäste auf Sachsens schönster Feste. Festung Königstein, 2020.
Viel früher als gedacht! Der Königstein in der Bronzezeit. Festung Königstein, 2021.

Abbildungsnachweise / Illustration credits

David Adam 78.3, 79.4
Thomas Eichberg 10.2
Festung Königstein gGmbH 30.2, 40.1, 41.2, 49.9, 50.2, 56.1
Steffen Füssel 56.1
Matthias Hultsch 33.7, 48.7, 50.1, 55.5, 76/77.1
Manchester City Galleries 64.1, 65.2
Peter Mauksch 6.1, 7.3, 9.1, 12.4, 17.4, 19.7, 20.8, 20.9, 21.10, 24.13, 25.16, 26.16, 26.17, 28.1, 30.1, 31.3, 32.5, 36.2, 37.3, 39.6, 42.1, 45.2, 45.3, 46.3, 47.4, 48.6, 51.1, 52/53.2, 55.4, 57.2, 59.2, 60.1, 61.2, 61.3, 63.1, 63.2, 71.1, 71.2, 72.3, 73.4, 74.1, 75.2
MHM Dresden 38.4, 39.5
National Gallery of Art, Washington DC 23.12
Hans Dieter Schaal 6.2, 16.2, 17.3, 24.14, 34.1, 36.1, 36.1, 44.1, 44.2, 67.3, 68.1, 69.2, 69.3
Verena Schaal 7.4
Armin Teufel 16.1, 31.4
Bernd Walther 14.1, 18.5, 18.6, 22.11, 25.15, 27.18, 54.3, 67.2
Silke Weichelt 40.1, 41.3, 48.8, 49.9